Jim King

THE HOLY SPIRIT

Common Sense and the Bible

OTHER BOOKS BY AUTHOR

Let's Glorify God

Missions in Crisis

Prayer: Common Sense and the Bible

THE HOLY SPIRIT

Common Sense and the Bible

Eric S. Fife

ZONDERVAN
PUBLISHING HOUSE
OF THE ZONDERVAN CORPORATION
GRAND RAPIDS, MICHIGAN 49506

THE HOLY SPIRIT: COMMON SENSE AND THE BIBLE
Copyright © 1978 by Eric S. Fife
Grand Rapids, Michigan

Library of Congress Cataloging in Publication Data

Fife, Eric S
    The Holy Spirit.

        1. Holy Spirit.   2. Pentecostalism. I. Title.
BT121.2.F47   231'.3   78-11751
ISBN 0-310-24341-6

Unless otherwise indicated, all Scriptures are taken from the *Revised Standard Version of the Bible*.

We are grateful to the following publishers for permission to use their Bible translations in our book:

The New English Bible. Copyright © 1961 and 1970 by the Delegates of the Oxford University Press and The Syndics of the Cambridge University Press.

The New Testament in Modern English by J. B. Phillips. Copyright © 1958, 1960, 1972 by J. B. Phillips. Printed by the Macmillan Company.

The Revised Standard Version. Copyright © 1946, 1952 and 1972 by Division of Christian Education of the National Council of Churches of Christ in the United States of America.

The New International Version: New Testament. Copyright © 1973 by New York Bible Society International. Published by the Zondervan Corporation.

Printed in the United States of America

To Hazel, Janet, and Brenda
whom I greatly neglected in
their childhood so that I could
minister to the youth of many
families in many countries

Contents

	Preface		11
	Foreword		13
	Introduction		15
1	The Personality of the Holy Spirit		17
2	The Holy Spirit and the Trinity		22
3	The Holy Spirit and Creation		25
	Creation of the Earth and Ocean	25	
	Creation of the Heavens	27	
	Creation of Animals and Vegetation	29	
	Creation of Man	30	
	Creation Conclusion	31	
4	The Attributes of the Holy Spirit		33
	Limitless Knowledge	36	
	The Spirit of Holiness	39	
	The Omnipotence of the Holy Spirit	43	
	The Holy Spirit and Love	45	
	The Unlimited Presence of the Holy Spirit	47	
5	The Holy Spirit and the Old Testament		50
6	The Holy Spirit and Common Grace		60
7	The Holy Spirit in the Gospels		64
	The Incarnation	65	
	The Baptism of Jesus Christ	68	
	The Death of Jesus Christ	72	
	The Resurrection of Jesus Christ	74	
8	The Holy Spirit and Pentecost		76
9	The Holy Spirit and the Apostolic Church		83
	The Change in the Disciples	84	
	The Message of the Apostles	89	
	The Spread of the Apostolic Church	91	
10	The Baptism of the Holy Spirit		95
11	The Fullness of the Holy Spirit		98
12	Spiritual Warfare		103
13	The Gifts of the Holy Spirit in General		107
	Are Spiritual Gifts for Today?	108	

9

	Spiritual Gifts and Natural Talents	112	
	Spiritual Gifts and Human Personalities	113	
14	The Gifts of the Holy Spirit and the Fruits of the Holy Spirit		116
15	Some Individual Spiritual Gifts		121
	Apostles	121	
	Prophets	124	
	Teachers	129	
	Miracle Workers	133	
	Healers	135	
	Helpers	138	
	Administrators	139	
	Tongues	140	
	Utterance of Wisdom and Utterance of Knowledge	152	
	Faith	154	
	Discerning of Spirits	154	
	Evangelists	155	
	Pastors and Teachers	157	
	Liberality	159	
16	Exorcism		163
	The Diagnosis	163	
	The Treatment	164	
	Some Dangers and Errors	164	
17	The Holy Spirit and Divine Guidance		167
18	The Strengths of the Charismatic Movement		170
19	The Weaknesses of the Charismatic Movement		176
20	A Sketch of the Charismatic Movement		183
	The Cumberland Presbyterian Church	185	
	Azusa Street	187	
	The Lutheran Story	189	
	The Roman Catholics	191	
	The Armenian Story	192	
	The Assemblies of God	195	
21	Conclusion		197
	Bibliography		201
	Indexes		205

Preface

My friend Eric Fife has written this book on the Holy Spirit with a single objective—and I think he has fulfilled his purpose—to center our attention on the Holy Spirit as the Third Person of the Godhead, and I am glad he has done this.

He takes us thoroughly, Scripture by Scripture, through all the Bible revelation of the Holy Spirit as the living Third Person of the Trinity, by whom the Father through the Son came into visible manifestation in creation and redemption, and by whom the Son is in our personal experience the Lord Jesus Christ dwelling in our hearts by faith. This Bible survey is of itself of great value when so many of us who are God's people know less of the Spirit who indwells us than we do of the Father and the Son.

Eric talks with us in simple style, often bringing in the personal, expressing his own viewpoints, and giving his own expositions, illustrated from incidents in his church and student ministry as former Missionary Director of the Inter-Varsity Christian Fellowship. He covers the various operations of the Spirit in our personal lives. He discusses questions so often asked about favorite Bible phrases such as "the baptism of the Spirit," "the filling of the Spirit," guidance by the Spirit, and the fruit and gifts of the Spirit.

In such a broad coverage he obviously cannot go deeply into Pauline details on each; and he knows that there are varieties of interpretation and conviction (in some of which he and I would say things differently!), and that will go for all readers who have a background in the Bible! Eric does not fail to speak out, sometimes caustically, especially along the line of the dangers of overemphasis, often through overenthusiasm for our "pet" convictions! I am especially happy that, as he moves toward his final chapters, he writes warmly and emphatically of the mighty workings of the Spirit in our day through what we usually speak of as the charismatic. Though neither he nor I have been brought by the same Spirit into those experiences, he rejoices in all that God is doing world-wide, and often in his own participation with them, including the new trends in public worship into liberty in song and praise in less structured forms. While he quotes from many authors, it is striking to me that more than any other he quotes from that wise and balanced "father" (now with the Lord) among the British Pentecostals, Donald Gee.

He finally presents us with the challenge of knowing for sure that we are each "baptized in the Spirit" and filled and endued by the Spirit, in whatever way He has manifested Himself to us in His fullness; and that we are big enough to rejoice and fellowship with all people of the Spirit. In his last word he takes us back to where he started—that is, with the Spirit Himself, not His gifts, fruit, or outworkings. We have a living union and fellowship with Him, and I believe this book will be the further confirmation to many of us that we are ourselves "the epistle of Christ, not written with ink, but with the Spirit of the living God."

Norman Grubb

Foreword

In the New Testament sense of that much maligned word, Eric
Fife is ecumenical, a Christian whose ministry has been international and interdenominational. A reverent and devoted
student of the Bible, he has served as Inter-Varsity's missionary
director, an English pastor, a popular conference speaker, and
a discerning observer of the church around the world. With
these credentials he has written a full-length doctrinal study,
not a dry, technical treatise, but a vibrant, down-to-earth examination of the person and work of the Holy Spirit. Studded
with personal experiences, this book aims to deepen the
reader's own experience. Thus, at the end of each chapter
there are questions to stimulate reflection.

As might be expected—and particularly so from Eric Fife—
controversial positions are taken and opinions advanced which
are not in accord with mainline American evangelicalism. Yet
this work has values which make it stimulating and profitable.

1. It highlights the towering importance of the Spirit's
   reality, personality, and activity.
2. It discusses virtually every essential aspect of the biblical disclosure regarding the Holy Spirit.
3. While the Spirit, of course, does not operate contrary
   to Scripture, this study recognizes His unpredictable
   freedom and sovereignty in all He does, calling to
   mind a statement by G. Campbell Morgan in his
   commentary on the Acts of the Apostles: "the moment
   we become mystified in the presence of the operations
   of the Spirit, we have reached the heart of truth. 'The

wind bloweth where it will, and thou hearest the voice thereof, but knowest not whence it cometh, and whither it goeth.' The moment in which any theologian or school of theology attempts to systematize the coming of the Spirit into human lives, in that moment they are excluding a score of His operations, and including only one."

4. It essays an objective appraisal of the charismatic movement, criticizing what Fife takes to be its weaknesses yet rejoicing that it has been a vitalizing force in countless lives and, Fife argues, in Christendom at large.

5. Above all, it prods us concerning our own relationship to the Holy Spirit.

Eric Fife says he has sought to build bridges where division and misunderstanding now exist in this crucial area of revelational truth. In my judgment he has succeeded.

Vernon Grounds

Introduction

My wife looked up from the dictionary she was studying and with a note of surprise in her voice remarked, "Do you know that the words 'charisma' and 'charismatic' are not in the dictionary?" I suggested that she look up the word "pentecostal." This word was also missing. I then checked the publication date of the dictionary. It was 1957, a little more than twenty years ago. Our discovery made me pursue the matter further by a visit to the public library. There I was able to check these omissions with a 1975 edition of the same dictionary I owned. I found the three words were in this recent edition with very good definitions. This is a clear indication that these words associated with the Holy Spirit had come into common secular usage in the past twenty years or less.

When I arrived in the United States in 1955, I was appalled at the lack of teaching on the Holy Spirit. Over a period of many years I endeavored to counteract this omission by preaching series of sermons on the person and work of the Holy Spirit, particularly at student conferences. Christian bookstores now have their shelves packed with books on the subject of the Holy Spirit. This fact made me reluctant to add to the avalanche. I would like to acknowledge the constant encouragement I received from Dr. Robert K. DeVries, of Zondervan Publishing House, who kept me committed to this task.

I have discovered several books, mostly old, that have dealt with such subjects as the Holy Spirit in creation, His personality and attributes, etc., but without exception these do not deal

15

with such subjects as the gifts of the Spirit, or the charismatic movement. On the other hand there are innumerable books that deal with aspects of the charismatic movement, but make little or no attempt to deal with the Holy Spirit, His attributes and His person. I have endeavored to rectify this. I trust I have succeeded.

My aim in this book has been to cover a fairly wide view of the subject, to write practically and simply, and at the same time keep within the bounds of sound theological thought. I pray and trust that some will gain information concerning the Holy Spirit, but more importantly that many will be led to appropriate the boundless resources of the Holy Spirit for their own lives.

I am greatly indebted to my wife Joan who has become my secretary, and who typed the first draft of this book. My daughter Janet who made invaluable editorial suggestions, and my eldest daughter Hazel Fife Pridgen who typed much of the final draft. I also wish to place on record my thanks for the helpfulness of Mr. Ed Viening, Senior Editor of the Zondervan Publishing House. The fact that the book was written in my home in Albuquerque, while my library was still in England, made the task more difficult and protracted. However, I was able to accomplish a considerable amount of research on the subject. All who read this book will not agree with all my views, but I have attempted to relate to the layman a balance of Scriptural truth which I feel is necessary, when so many are confused and perplexed at what is happening today.

1

The Personality of the Holy Spirit

We are living in a day in which we find an unparalleled interest in the gifts and power of the Spirit. Indeed, it is hard to find a Christian bookstore that does not have its shelves crammed with books on the subject. I have read as many of these books as is reasonably possible, and I find a strange omission. People seem to be far more interested in what the Holy Spirit does than who He is. Like the Corinthian Church the more sensational the work, the greater the interest shown. I discover little interest in what the Holy Spirit is like. The neglect no longer surprises me. The church of Christ has for many years been more interested in man than in God, more in the experience of Christians than in the characteristics of God. In a phrase, it is more man-centered than God-centered.

No man, church, or religion rises above its concept of God. The reason why there is so frequently shallowness in Holy Spirit-oriented Christians is that they have been more concerned with repeating testimonies of their own experience than with sound teaching about the character of the Holy Spirit.

The true understanding of the personality of the Holy Spirit is covered by so many layers of ignorance, indifference, and prejudice, that it would take a prolonged effort to scrape them off and to cast them away. It reminds me of some old masterpieces that have lost their glorious luster because centuries of accumulated filth and neglect have been allowed to gather. It takes bold but sensitive hands to remove the encrustation so that the picture can be seen in all its original beauty. A. W. Tozer has written that "the essence of idolatry is the enter-

17

tainment of thoughts about God that are unworthy of Him."[1] By this definition most books and sermons about the Holy Spirit are idolatrous.

****

In my opinion this neglect of the nature of God the Father, Son, and Holy Spirit has undermined every aspect of the work of the church. C. H. Spurgeon once wrote that "the higher a man grows in grace, the lower he sinks in his own estimation." We must always remember that God's supreme purpose in the world is not to save man, it is to glorify Himself.

In thinking of the personality of the Holy Spirit the most obvious and important truth to stress is that He is a person. There is still a tendency to think and talk of Him as being an impersonal power, an it. To fully comprehend the nature of God is impossible for fallen man. Although we seek to understand Him, and the Scripture sheds light on the subject, we must begin by realizing that it is not possible to understand Him perfectly. These things are as much beyond the mind of man as the beauty of a sunset is beyond the understanding of a jellyfish. Although we may not fully understand, it is our duty and pleasure to comprehend as much as has been revealed for us in the Scriptures. When Jesus promised that the Holy Spirit would descend upon man, He seemed to particularly stress the fact of His personality by the use of the personal pronoun. "The Father . . . will give you another Counselor, to be with you for ever, even the Spirit of truth, whom the world cannot receive. . . . you know *him* for *he* is with you, and will be in you" (John 14:16-17, italics mine). "When the Spirit of truth comes, *he* will guide you into all the truth; for *he* will not speak on *his* own authority, but whatever *he* hears *he* will speak, and *he* will declare to you the things that are to come. *He* will glorify *me*" (John 16:13-14, italics mine).

Being a person implies having a personality with the capac-

[1]A. W. Tozer, *The Knowledge of the Holy* (Harrisburg, Pa.: Christian Publications, Inc., 1975).

ity for intelligence, love, anger, and grief. This is graphically confirmed by the prophet Isaiah, "But they rebelled and grieved his holy Spirit; therefore he turned to be their enemy, and himself fought against them" (Isa. 63:10). It is imperative for us to understand the Holy Spirit's nature as completely as possible if we are to fully enjoy His liberating power within us. Only God has a perfect personality. As G. Campbell Morgan has written, "God is not a magnified man, rather it may be said that man is a limited God."[2]

Because the Holy Spirit is a person, we can and indeed must treat Him as a person. In that fact lies the possibility of comfort, guidance, and knowledge such as is impossible for unregenerate man to comprehend. It also has within it the seeds of possible disaster, as we have seen in Isaiah 63. This can also be seen in Acts 5:1-6. Ananias and Sapphira lied concerning their giving and were stricken by death, not because their gift was inadequate, but because of their premeditated lying. Incidently, that passage gives further weight to the deity of the Holy Spirit; verse 3 refers to lying to the Holy Spirit, and verse 4 equates this with lying to God. "Ananias, why has Satan filled your heart to lie to the Holy Spirit. . . ? You have not lied to men but to God." "How is it that you have agreed together to tempt the Spirit of the Lord?" Peter asks in verse 9.

We learn from the letter to the Hebrews that the Holy Spirit is a person who can be outraged. "A man who has violated the law of Moses dies without mercy at the testimony of two or three witnesses. How much worse punishment do you think will be deserved by the man who has spurned the Son of God, and profaned the blood of the covenant by which he was sanctified, and outraged the spirit of grace?" (Heb. 10:28-29). This sense of outrage is wholly in keeping with the One whom Jesus Christ said "will glorify me."

When Stephen made his striking defense before the high priest just before his own death, he accused the Sanhedrin:

[2]G. Campbell Morgan, *The Spirit of God* (London: Westminster City Publishing Co., n.d.) p. 23.

"You stiff-necked people, uncircumcised in heart and ears, you always resist the Holy Spirit" (Acts 7:51). His earthly reward for teaching this was death by stoning: ugly and protracted as stones thudded into flesh. The Jews did not appreciate being told this truth. We also may recoil at the thought that we are capable of resisting the Spirit. Many Christians grieve Him by their actions; Stephen's enemies acted in what was to them perfect sincerity, but to God almighty it was blind prejudice. "They will put you out of the synagogues; indeed, the hour is coming when whoever kills you will think he is offering service to God. And they will do this because they have not known the Father, nor me" (John 16:2-3).

Our Lord while on earth taught that it is possible to blaspheme against the Holy Spirit: ". . . the blasphemy against the Spirit will not be forgiven" (Matt. 12:31-32). We know that because the Holy Spirit is a person He can be grieved, and He can be blasphemed against. The ultimate sin against the Spirit is to deliberately and finally refuse Him.

If we were to learn that the President of the United States or the Queen of Great Britain was going to stay in our home, we would be honored to the point of embarrassment. We would doubtless seek details of their diets and wishes so that we could please them as much as possible. Should we do less to please the royal guest, the Holy Spirit, who lives in our lives?

Let us take time to absorb the main characteristics of the almighty Spirit:

1. He is a person (John 16:13-14)
2. He is God (Acts 5:3-4)
3. He is intelligent (1 Cor. 2:10-11)
4. He has the capacity to love (1 John 4:8)
5. He can be outraged (Heb. 10:28-29)
6. He can be resisted (Acts 7:51)
7. He can be blasphemed against (Matt. 12:31)
8. He can be lied to (Acts 5:9)
9. He can be grieved (Eph. 4:30)
10. He can be quenched (1 Thess. 5:19)

Now let us pause to digest the glorious fact that although

20

these things are all true of the Holy Spirit, He is willing to live within us. Few truths can transform a life as these truths can when they are assimilated. What task or duty can be mundane or insignificant if God almighty is living within our personalities? What service can be too difficult if He is working in us and through us? How careful we must be to avoid offending this heavenly guest!

We should indeed be glad and delighted that the Holy Spirit is a person who understands us, loves us, and heaps His benefits upon us day by day.

FOR DISCUSSION

1. Do Christians display more interest in the person of the Holy Spirit or the gifts of the Holy Spirit?

2. Are Christians more interested in who the Holy Spirit is, or what He does?

3. Are Christians, as a rule, God-centered or man-centered?

4. Is the Holy Spirit a power or a person?

5. Can we perfectly understand the person of the Holy Spirit?

6. Quote a Bible passage that emphasizes that the Holy Spirit is a person.

7. In which book of the Bible do we read that Stephen accused people of resisting the Holy Spirit?

8. Name seven characteristics of the Holy Spirit.

2

The Holy Spirit and the Trinity

The subject of the Trinity is no problem to some Christians. This is not necessarily because of superior knowledge or spiritual insight; it may rather reveal how little they have thought about the subject. It is sad that among the millions who call themselves Bible-believing, born-again Christians (many of whom delight in telling how many modern versions of the Bible they possess), only a tiny minority have given much thought to the nature of God.

I well remember an incident which occurred when I had been a Christian for ten years; I met a member of a small and heretical sect. I thought I was fairly well equipped to counter his arguments until he asked what my authority was for believing in the Trinity. I answered him as best I could, but knew that I had been a miserable failure. The incident had one happy outcome; it drove me back to my Bible and study books in an attempt to understand more of the nature of God and the Trinity.

The Bible states the Trinity as a fact but does not explain it, not because the Bible is limited but because our intellects are. Can one be three, and three be one? The Unitarian makes a feeble and vain effort to wrap his mind around the Trinity and eventually finds that his mind has no God. The Muslim hears about the Trinity and immediately brands Christians as polytheists, having three Gods. The Bible teaches the Trinity in unity. We must accept this by faith and remember that if we had complete proof there would be no room for faith. Nor must we think of a divine, unending committee meeting, but rather of three persons in one, with one will.

To explain this, man has fallen back on many analogies, such as that of water. It is a liquid which, when heated, becomes a vapor. When cooled it becomes a solid, ice. This analogy is not adequate to explain the mystery, however. All analogies can be dangerous, because all fall so far short of the real thing. The subject is just too exalted for man to understand. Walter Chalmers Smith wrote well of God's incomprehensibility and of our difficulty in understanding God:

> Immortal, invisible, God only wise
> In light inaccessible hid from our eyes...
>
> Great Father of Glory, pure Father of Light,
> Thine angels adore Thee, all veiling their sight;
> All laud we would render, O help us to see
> 'Tis only the splendour of light hideth Thee.

The first hint of plurality in the Godhead is seen as early as Genesis 1:26: "Then God said 'Let *us* make man in *our* own image, after *our* likeness'" (italics mine). The thought broadens considerably when we read of the baptism of Jesus: "And when Jesus was baptized, he went up immediately from the water, and behold, the heavens were opened and he saw the Spirit of God descending like a dove, and alighting on him; and lo, a voice from heaven, saying, 'This is my beloved Son, with whom I am well pleased'" (Matt. 3:16-17). Here we are confronted by the three Persons of the Trinity at the same time.

In the course of His life and teaching ministry Jesus referred often to the Father, and also to the Holy Spirit. These references culminated in His last instructions: "Go therefore and make disciples of all nations, baptizing them in the name of the Father and of the Son and of the Holy Spirit" (Matt. 28:19).

The Holy Spirit is referred to as the Third Person of the Trinity. This in no sense implies an inferior status. In John

15:26 Jesus declares that "... when the Counselor comes, whom I shall send to you from the Father, even the Spirit of truth, who proceeds from the Father...." God the Son was begotten, not created, in contrast to all other beings such as men and angels who were created. The Holy Spirit was not created or begotten but proceeds from the Father.

Instead of concentrating on the wonderful works of the Holy Spirit and His gifts, let us determine to praise Him for who He is: a person, a member of the Trinity, from everlasting to everlasting.

FOR DISCUSSION

1. The subject of the Holy Spirit and the Trinity raises no problem for many Christians. Why is this?

2. Does the Bible teach us anything about the Trinity and the Holy Spirit?

3. Does the Bible completely describe the Trinity?

4. Supply at least one Bible verse that suggests the existence of the Trinity.

5. The Holy Spirit is described as the Third Person of the Trinity. Does this infer an inferior status?

6. Why do we associate the Trinity with the ordinance of baptism?

3

The Holy Spirit and Creation

In a later chapter we will look at the work of the Holy Spirit in the Acts of the Apostles. There is a real danger in thinking (if only subconsciously) that Pentecost was the beginning of the work of the Holy Spirit, forgetting that He was involved in all facets of creation. God certainly does not satisfy all our curiosity concerning creation, for the purpose of the Bible is to reveal Christ in His glory, not to give a detailed and scientific description of all events.

CREATION OF THE EARTH AND OCEAN

In Genesis 1:1,2 we read, "In the beginning God created the heavens and the earth. The earth was without form and void, and darkness was upon the face of the deep; and the Spirit of God was moving over the face of the waters."

In the light of modern trends it is important to notice that the Bible begins with God and not with man. John Owen, writing of the Trinity in connection with creation, writes that "every person (of the Trinity) therefore, is the author of every work of God, because each person is God . . . ."[1] Martin Luther, writing in reference to Genesis 1:2 says, "Consequently the Christian Church on this point displays a strong unity that in this description is to be found the mystery of the Holy Trinity." It is of more than usual significance to note that the plurality of the

[1]John Owen, *The Holy Spirit* (Grand Rapids: Sovereign Grace Publishers, n.d.), p. 93.

Godhead is mentioned as early as the first two verses of the Bible.

The Scripture (Gen. 1:2) goes on to say that "the Spirit of God was moving over the face of the waters." The New English Bible speaks of a "mighty wind that swept over the surface of the water." This might appear to be a discrepancy, since the Revised Standard Version says the activity was by the Spirit of God, and the New English Bible talks about "a mighty wind." This discrepancy disappears when we remember that the word used can be translated as breath, wind, or spirit. It is helpful to remember that when the outpouring of the Spirit took place at Pentecost, "a sound came from heaven like the rush of a mighty wind" (Acts 2:2). Wind is only one symbol of the Holy Spirit; others are breath, a dove, oil, and fire.

It is to David's credit that, though he had virtually no revelation of God through the Scriptures, he saw the hand of God in every part of creation and in every circumstance. That this is the only appropriate reaction can be seen from Romans 1:20: "Ever since the creation of the world his invisible nature, namely, his eternal power and deity, has been clearly perceived in the things that have been made. *So they are without excuse.*" In the life of Jesus Christ some saw His miracles as just that. In John 2 the master of the marriage feast was the first to express wonder at the quality of the wine that Christ had made from water, but the effect on the disciples was different. "This, the first of his signs, Jesus did at Cana in Galilee, and manifested his glory; *and his disciples believed in him*" (John 2:11, italics mine).

We see His ways and His works in Scripture. David, as a shepherd, was closer to nature, and he saw the footprint of God everywhere. It is quite an experience to see the glory of an untrod alpine meadow with its countless varieties of colored flowers, and to know that they appeared for centuries before they were seen by man. It is awe-inspiring to see beneath the surface of the ocean the wonders of the deep: the brain and antler corals, or the faintly-threatening beauty of a kelp bed, with stems one hundred feet or more long gracefully waving in the current as if in some slow-motion minuet. It is glorious to see the wonder of a desert sunset. There is only one response from those who know the living God: "O LORD, our Lord, how majestic is thy name in all the earth!" (Ps. 8:1). David was not only observant of the earth but also the sky, which he knew and loved so well. Then there is the overwhelming beauty under the sea, largely unseen and unknown to man until the invention of the scuba tank about thirty years ago. Even then the reaction of those who see these spectacles is much like that of the five hundred fed by Jesus Christ. Most of the people were excited by the miracle, all enjoyed eating the bread, but only a few had their eyes opened to see in it the glory of God. For the unimpressed, "They are without excuse" rings like a death knell.

This description of His activity in creation is not that of an instantaneous act but of a continuing presence, the Spirit hovering over the deep. This activity of the Holy Spirit in creation is merely one more evidence of His limitless power, since it is only God who can create. Man can construct out of existing matter but has no power to create out of nothing. The word "create" is used loosely in our day; even a hair style is described as a "creation" by so and so. Of course it is not a creation; it is an arrangement.

CREATION OF THE HEAVENS

The creative power and ministry of the Holy Spirit is not confined to the earth and seas but involves much more, including the heavens. "By the word of the LORD the heavens were made, and all their host by the breath of his mouth. He gathered the waters of the sea as in a bottle; he put the deeps in storehouses" (Ps. 33:6-7). Job was enlightened enough to state that "by his wind the heavens were made fair" (Job 26:13). Job went on to say that this is by no means the totality of His creative power. "Lo, these are but the outskirts of his ways; and how small a whisper do we hear of him! But the thunder of his power who can understand?" (Job 26:14). The response of the man who has insight into these creative works of God the Holy Spirit is one of wonder and reverence. For example, "Let all the earth fear the Lord, let all the inhabitants of the world stand in awe of him!" Immediately following is the statement that "by the word of the LORD the heavens were made, and all their host by the breath of his mouth." Whoever wrote Psalm 33, and there are good reasons to believe it was David, its response is the only valid one from finite man coming face to face with the handiwork of the infinite God. A similar sequence is found in Psalm 8: "When I look at thy heavens, the work of thy fingers, the moon and the stars which thou hast established... O LORD, our Lord, how majestic is thy name in all the earth!" (vv. 3,9).

Continuing our theme of creation, we read, "Thou hast made the moon to mark the seasons; the sun knows its time for setting" (Ps. 104:19). Remembering the limited scientific knowledge there was at the time of the writing of this Psalm, we who are the possessors of greater knowledge and insight must recognize the fact that we have a corresponding and greater responsibility. The space shots that are a common part of today's life are possible because the movement of celestial bodies is utterly reliable to a measurement of time hidden from the psalmist: measurements can be made months and years in advance for space shots and the exploration of the moon and Mars. Small wonder that in ancient times men regarded the sun, the moon, and the hosts of the heavens as objects of worship. Instead of worshiping the Creator, they worshiped His creations. "Therefore they are without excuse."

Even in our day, the supposedly enlightened people who by the millions study horoscopes and believe that their lives are influenced by them, "are without excuse." How insistent is the Scripture that the heavens and the bodies in them are made by God; man's only appropriate response is the one which we have seen comes like a great refrain: "Bless the LORD, O my soul! O LORD my God, thou art very great!" (Ps. 104:1). Indeed, the whole of Psalm 104 is one sustained testimony to the glory of God as revealed in nature: "who coverest thyself with light as with a garment" (v. 2), and "who makest the clouds thy chariot" (v. 3). If we study that Psalm more fully other things will come to our attention.

In our dealing with the heavenly hosts our thoughts almost immediately turn to Job 38:7: ". . . the morning stars sang together, and all the sons of God shouted for joy." Can stars sing for joy? For centuries this was considered to be poetic license rather than an actual possibility. We now live in a world in which men, formerly intoxicated by their own knowledge, confess that the concept of a sharp division between light and sound was a view based upon ignorance, and is scientifically unsound. We send voice messages along laser beams of light, and microwaves can split a rock. In other words both sound and light are the product of vibrations of varying types, so what we see as star light can easily be heard by beings whose ears are attuned to receive messages beyond the range of human hearing. Indeed, outer space is examined not only by telescope but also by radio telescopes.

CREATION OF ANIMALS AND VEGETATION

If God the Spirit created the earth, the oceans, and the heavens, does that exhaust His creative ministry? By no means. Indeed, Psalm 104 can be regarded as a commentary upon the first chapter of Genesis. This Psalm deals with the creation and preservation of animals. ". . . springs . . . give drink to every beast of the field" (v. 11). Then follows a catalog of creatures: "The wild asses . . . the birds . . . the cattle . . . the stork . . . the wild goats . . . the lions. . . ." The psalmist asserts that God alone can provide water in the right quantity for the animals' needs. Despite modern technology we are still completely dependent upon God, as we are reminded almost annually by a succession of floods and droughts throughout the earth. In verse 30 there is at least a hint that the Holy Spirit is instrumental in the growth of the very grass for food: "When thou sendest forth thy Spirit, they are created; and thou renewest the face of the ground." And in verse 14, "Thou dost cause the grass to grow for the cattle, and plants for man to cultivate, that he may bring forth food from the earth." This is further strengthened by a negative thought from another source: "The grass withers, the flower fades, when the breath of the LORD blows upon it; surely the people is grass" (Isa. 40:7).

If we begin to see something of the fullness of the Holy Spirit as revealed by His mighty creative work, we see Him as a Person of unlimited power, with the ability to produce an astonishing variety of beauty, on whom the whole of creation depends.

CREATION OF MAN

"Then the LORD God formed man of dust from the ground, and breathed into his nostrils the breath of life; and man became a living being" (Gen. 2:7), and "The Spirit of God has made me, and the breath of the Almighty gives me life" (Job 33:4). The high point of creation was the making of man; again it is significant that the Holy Spirit was involved.

Genesis 1 tells us that God made man in His own image. What is meant by the fact that man is made in the image of God? Before the Fall many of the attributes of God were enjoyed by man. After the Fall some of these attributes were defaced by sin and disobedience, but always there was an opportunity of redemption: "He made him a living soul," as distinct from the animals. Another attribute that man received from God was that of authority. In Psalm 8 we read that "God . . . dost crown him with glory and honor. Thou hast given him dominion over the works of thy hands; thou hast put all things under his feet, all sheep and oxen, and also the beasts of the field, the birds of the air, and the fish of the sea" (vv. 5-8). It is strange that through an erroneous translation the significance of this Psalm is so frequently lost. As has been pointed out elsewhere, David sees the heavens at night, is impressed by the stars and moon, attributes them to the work of "God's fingers," and in view of the vastness of heaven utters the question, What is man? Then comes the triumphant answer. Man is *not* insignificant (as many have interpreted the Psalm as saying). The glorious truth is that "thou hast made him little less than God" (v. 5). David goes on to enlarge on the dominion man has over nature. We only have to visit the circus and the zoo to see elephants, lions, tigers, and whales under the dominion of man. Great though the authority of man is, it is to be stressed that authority was delegated to man from God. It is not an authority that was an inherent part of man's characteristics; God *gave* him dominion. This is of course in contrast to God's authority, which is eternal, unlimited, and can never be reduced by the process of subtraction.

We noted that the Son was not created but begotten, and the Spirit was not created but proceeds. Of all creatures and beings, including angels, that were created by God, man is at the top of the list. How tragic that in his fallen state he can control all beings but himself!

CREATION CONCLUSION

The point of the Genesis account is that there was chaos and darkness, and the Holy Spirit was present bringing order, beauty, and light out of it all. "In the beginning was the Word." John, writing thousands of years after Genesis, begins with "In the beginning," but almost hurries on to give the preeminence not to creation but to the *Creator.*

"In the beginning God created the heavens and the earth. The earth was without form and void and darkness was upon the face of the deep." This is a bleak picture and appears even bleaker in the New English Bible, which reads, "the earth was without form and void, with darkness over the face of the abyss." Here is a picture of desolation; not the type of desolation that is the result of a calamity, such as an earthquake, but rather the desolation that exists in a piece of rough stone before a skilled sculptor begins his work of fashioning beauty out of ugliness. And still He is performing this work today, fashioning beauty and holiness out of the wreck of men's lives.

Once again let us remember that the powerful Person who was the cause of creation is the same Person who resides in those who believe in Jesus Christ. As certainly as He brought order and beauty out of darkness and chaos in creation, so, just as certainly, He brings peace and beauty to those who bid Him to exercise His full ministry in their lives.

FOR DISCUSSION

1. Was Pentecost the beginning of the work of the Holy Spirit?
2. Where is the first reference in the Bible to the Holy Spirit in creation?
3. Give at least three symbols of the Holy Spirit that are found in the Bible.
4. Name at least one thing that we should see because of the miracles performed by God.
5. Give a Bible verse that refers to the creation of the heavens.
6. Do space shots tell us anything about the movement of celestial bodies?
7. Where does a Psalm attribute the growth of grass to the Holy Spirit?
8. Where do we read "The Spirit of God has made me"?
9. What is one thing that man cannot control?

4

The Attributes of the Holy Spirit

When guests come to stay with us, it is natural to want to know what they are like. We know that they have individual personalities and that each is different from everyone else.

We have discussed the fact that the Holy Spirit is a person, and that He is a member of the Trinity. This should tell us something about what He is like. A person reveals much of himself by the way he behaves; in the case of a creative person, by the quality of what he produces. Paul argues that even without scriptural revelation, God is clearly revealed by what He created in nature. "Ever since the creation of the world his invisible nature, namely, his eternal power and deity, has been clearly perceived in the things that have been made. So they are without excuse; for although they knew God they did not honor him as God or give thanks to him" (Rom. 1:20-21).

I have already commented on the fact that we are living in an age when even evangelicals know little about God. We are so engrossed with ourselves, our work, and our methods that we are far too busy to think seriously about God. We are so occupied with what we think is urgent that we don't have time to think about what is important.

The supreme purpose of the Bible is to reveal God. The supreme purpose of Satan is to make us think of anything but God, and he often tempts us to become more engrossed in God's work than in God Himself. Thus we major on minor points, neglecting the major ones. Often the good is the enemy of the best. It is important to know that the Holy Spirit has been so clearly revealed in the Scriptures, in creation, and by

Jesus Christ, that we too are without excuse if we withhold from Him the recognition and honor that are His due. This is a solemn thought. Indeed, many believe that to ignore the Holy Spirit is the one unforgivable sin. "Whoever blasphemes against the Holy Spirit *never* has forgiveness, but is guilty of an eternal sin" (Mark 3:29, italics mine). This is one of Jesus Christ's most challenging utterances and has caused heartache to many.

For example, John Bunyan and William Cowper were both convinced that they had committed the "unforgivable sin." John Bunyan overcame this feeling of guilt as demonstrated by *Grace Abounding* and *Pilgrim's Progress.* William Cowper suffered through much of his life from depression which at times developed into mania. Whether his theological views caused his emotional problems, or his emotional problems shaped his theological convictions it is impossible to say. He did write such glorious hymns as, "God moves in a mysterious way," "O for a closer walk with God," and also, "There is a fountain filled with blood." The unpardonable sin is not an isolated act or utterance, however, but a constantly defiant attitude that rejects the Light that is offered and prefers the darkness. And the text does underline the importance of the work of the Holy Spirit.

In past centuries men, notably the Puritans, preached and wrote about the attributes of God. As a consequence of their knowledge of the holy God they saw their own deficiencies, and this inevitably led to true humility. It has been asserted that "no man can at the same time give the impression that he is clever, and that Jesus Christ is mighty to save." This is an overstatement, but it certainly contains the seeds of a principle that our generation must know if they are to please God and see revival.

Whenever a man came face to face with the Almighty, the result was an awe and reverence such as is not seen today. When God revealed Himself to Paul on the Damascus road Paul fell on his face in the dust. Of all men who knew Jesus during His earthly life none was so intimate as the apostle

John; yet when, as a prisoner on the island of Patmos, he had a vision of the glorified Son of man, he fell at His feet as one dead (Rev. 1:17).

There is a marked contrast between past centuries, when godly men preached and wrote about the attributes of God, and our own day, when the diet is much more likely to be ghost-written biographies of pop stars or athletes. These often are interesting and entertaining, and they can be instructive. However, they are a poor substitute for the study of God Himself, and I think this accounts in large measure for our lack of humility and brokenness, and for the flippant thinking about God that is typical of our age.

I have stressed the unity of the Trinity. As the Third Person of the Trinity the Holy Spirit is not a junior partner. I must go much further and emphasize that every attribute of God the Father is also an attribute of the Holy Spirit. This is not merely an academic or theoretic matter, but is of enormous practical significance. If the Holy Spirit has a number of attributes, and if He is living in each Christian, He does not leave these attributes behind when He takes up residence in us. What a glorious thought that the unlimited God brings His own attributes into each of us! Salvation means that the sum of all these attributes is in us, and is shining through us.

I have said that there is a neglect of writing and reading about the attributes of God. If we narrow the subject and consider the attributes of the Holy Spirit, it will be seen that we are indeed in a barren wilderness of teaching. Even the great preachers and writers who in times past have dealt with the attributes of God seem not to have dealt with the attributes of God the Holy Spirit.

This is understandable because, of the flood of books on the Holy Spirit in recent years, this silence on the subject is inexcusable. So far as I can discover even the Puritans did not deal with this subject as often as might be expected; even if they did, comparatively few read the Puritans today.

Webster's New World Dictionary defines an attribute as "a characteristic or quality of a thing," and there is an area of overlap between the personality of the Holy Spirit and His characteristics. However, we shall see that by focusing our attention upon several of His characteristics we not merely enlarge our knowledge, but see more clearly the greatness of the gift that God has given in the person of the Holy Spirit.

LIMITLESS KNOWLEDGE

The technical theological term for this is omniscience. In an age when there has been an explosion of knowledge, it is all the more important to stress the limitless knowledge of the Holy Spirit in order to restore a right perspective. The Bible has many scathing things to say about man and his knowledge. In one sense knowledge is like money in that it is neither good nor evil, but can easily become a substitute for God. Paul, an intellectual, had a great deal to say about the limitations of human wisdom. "The world did not know God through wisdom" (1 Cor. 1:21). "You must no longer live as the Gentiles do, in the futility of their minds" (Eph. 4:17). Or, as Phillips graphically paraphrases the verse, "Do not live any longer the futile lives of Gentiles. For they live in a world of shadows."

Paul, writing to the Corinthians, expresses himself thus: "The wisdom of this world is folly with God," and again, "The Lord knows that the thoughts of the wise are futile" (1 Cor. 3:19,20). Let us be clear that there is no virtue in ignorance; the Bible nowhere suggests that there is. But neither is there virtue in human knowledge. If this appears to be a contradiction it must be remembered that philosophy is concerned with ideas *about* God, while the Bible's concern is communication *with* God. We only communicate with God on His terms and in accord with His revelation. Jesus made it clear that spiritual truths often are hidden from the wise and are revealed to children. This is, at least in part, because a child more easily has an uncluttered, simple faith and a sense of need. These are two indispensable ingredients if we are to know God.

The Bible states that "the Spirit searches everything, even the depths of God. . . . So also no one comprehends the thoughts of God except the Spirit of God" (1 Cor. 2:10-11). In this age of computers and space travel, when man is intoxicated by his own achievements, we need to remind ourselves that the whole sum of human knowledge can never bring us to God.

There are no secrets hidden from the Holy Spirit, and Jesus Christ has told us that He is our divine instructor: "When the Spirit of truth comes, he will guide you into all the truth; for he will not speak on his own authority, but whatever he hears he will speak, and he will declare to you the things that are to come. He will glorify me" (John 16:13-14).

Small wonder that Paul exclaims, "' . . . no eye has seen, nor ear heard, nor the heart of man conceived, what God has prepared for those who love him,' God has revealed to us through the Spirit. For the Spirit searches everything, even the depths of God. For what person knows a man's thoughts except the spirit of the man which is in him? So also no one comprehends the thoughts of God except the Spirit of God" (1 Cor. 2:9-11). This is not a theme that crops up suddenly in the New Testament; it runs through the entire Scripture. Isaiah, writing about the Messiah who was to come centuries later, says, "And the Spirit of the LORD shall rest upon him, the spirit of wisdom and understanding, the spirit of counsel and might, the spirit of knowledge and the fear of the LORD" (Isa. 11:2). No wonder that the apostle James writes, "If any of you lacks wisdom, let him ask God, who gives to all men generously and without reproaching, and it will be given him" (James 1:5). We have within our personalities, every moment, the supreme Counselor from whom not one iota of knowledge is hidden. This recognition should transform our attitude to the whole of life and Christian service. If an academic or a musician has studied under some great old master, how proud he is to make it known! It is wonderful that we can name among our instructors the greatest instructor who ever lived, the Holy Spirit who has all knowledge. When you next feel unqualified and insufficient to face a person or a task, take time to reflect that the Holy Spirit can guide you to truths unknown to "think tanks."

As we thrill at God's provision for our instruction and guidance let us also note that no matter how good a Christian other people think us to be, the Spirit of God knows not merely our actions but also the thoughts and intents of our heart. This does not mean that He is God's "resident policeman," but He is our Comforter who can be grieved by disobedience and who loathes phoniness. What a comfort to know that Satan cannot bring any sin of ours to light that the Holy Spirit has not already known and dealt with.

How wonderful to dwell upon the Spirit who has limitless knowledge. He has no need to increase his knowledge. We hope and expect that for us knowledge and wisdom are things that we will accumulate. When a young person speaks arrogantly we say, "He is immature; he will grow out of it." For the Spirit of God no such progress is necessary, and no one can be His instructor. The prophet Isaiah wrote, "Who has directed the Spirit of the LORD, or as his counselor has instructed him? Whom did he consult for his enlightenment, and who taught him the path of justice, and taught him knowledge, and showed him the way of understanding?" (Isa. 40:13-14). The limitless knowledge of the Holy Spirit was His before the foundation of the earth. He has no need to learn, and indeed He cannot learn. Omniscience is concerned not merely with quantity of knowledge but also with quality; the Holy Spirit has perfect knowledge. As A. W. Tozer has pointed out, "He never discovers anything and can never be surprised." We may believe all this in theory but still deny it in practice. Why should we be harrassed and worried when we have One living in us who is the fount of all knowledge, who knows all the present and all the past? We would do well to take time to allow this fact to soak into our minds and into our beings. If in the eyes of the world we are considered to be more intelligent than some, let us remember that to enter the kingdom we must become as babes; but having become babes we are led into knowledge and wisdom hidden from those who are called clever. There lives in us He who is the beginning and end of wisdom and knowledge.

Isaiah the prophet expresses much concerning the Holy Spirit: " 'From the time it came to be I have been there.' And now the Lord GOD has sent me and his Spirit" (Isa. 48:16).

Paul emphasizes a practical aspect of the work of the Spirit in and for the believer. "Likewise the Spirit helps us in our weakness; for we do not know how to pray as we ought, but the Spirit himself intercedes for us with sighs too deep for words . . . because the Spirit intercedes for the saints according to the will of God" (Rom. 8:26-27).

THE SPIRIT OF HOLINESS

How do I begin to write about the holiness of God? Nothing in the experience of the writer or of the reader equips him to get beyond the outer fringes of God's holiness. It is nowhere described in the Scripture; how can language deal with a dimension that is so utterly alien to the experience and the mind of man? The Scripture does not leave us completely in the dark, however. As has been mentioned elsewhere, the apostle John was given at least a partial glimpse of the glory and holiness of God while he was on the island of Patmos. He had been accustomed to walking the byways of Israel with Jesus during His earthly ministry, dressed in homespun garments and sharing sleeping quarters. John had seen glimpses of His glory; he first believed when he saw water turned into wine at Cana, and there were many other such experiences. It is characteristic of John that in his own gospel he is silent concerning the most dramatic experience of Jesus' life he was privileged to attend. "Jesus took with him Peter and James and John his brother, and led them up a high mountain apart. And he was transfigured before them, and his face shone like the sun, and his garments became white as light. . . . . He was still speaking, when lo, a bright cloud overshadowed them, and a voice from the cloud said, 'This is my beloved Son, with whom I am well pleased; listen to Him' " (Matt. 17:1-2,5). John was given yet a further revelation on the isle of Patmos. "His head and his hair were white as white wool, white as snow; his eyes were like a flame of fire, his feet were like burnished bronze, refined as in a furnace, and his voice was like the sound of many waters..." (Rev. 1:14,15).

I hate noise, but the sound of mighty waves has always had a great attraction for me. This phrase, "His voice was like the sound of many waters," has meant far more to me since I visited Niagara Falls. To see the high-flung pall that looks like steam, but is in fact spray, and then to hear that indescribable roar! The sound of many waters at Niagara is noise that is heavenly harmony. It is truly awesome.

"In his right hand he held seven stars, from his mouth issued a sharp two-edged sword, and his face was like the sun shining in full strength" (Rev. 1:16). The result was predictable: "I fell at his feet as though dead" (v.17).

One of the problems of true understanding of the holiness of God is that "man shall not see me and live" (Exod. 33:20). Moses asked to see the glory of the Lord; God promised that on the mountain top He would make His goodness pass before Moses, and that Moses would see the glory of God pass by (Exod. 33:18-23). When Moses climbed the mountain with the tablets of stone, "the LORD descended in the cloud and stood with him there, and proclaimed the name of the LORD" (Exod. 34:4-5).

Moses, wonderfully privileged, could see the glory of God, could view His presence in a cloud, and could hear His voice, *but he could not look on God and live.* Even though Moses did not come face to face with the living God, we learn that "Moses did not know that the skin of his face shone because he had been talking with God. And when Aaron and all the people of Israel saw Moses, behold, the skin of his face shone, and they were afraid to come near him" (Exod. 34:29-30). The meaning of holiness is "set apart," and places and utensils that are used exclusively for the service of the Lord are called holy. This is only a pale reflection of the set-apartness that characterizes a holy God. Holiness means the separation of God from creation and above it. It shows the utter supremacy of God. "Who is like thee, O LORD, among the gods? Who is like thee, majestic in holiness, terrible in glorious deeds, doing wonders?" (Exod. 15:11). Holiness is a term that not only speaks of separateness and glory but also of moral excellence, and God's freedom from all limitations of His moral perfection.

Eternal Light! eternal light!
How pure the soul must be,
When placed within Thy searching sight,
It shrinks not, but with calm delight
Can live and look on Thee.

The spirits that surround Thy throne
May bear the burning bliss;
But that is surely theirs alone,
Since they have never, never known
A fallen world like this.

There is a way for man to rise
To that sublime abode:
An offering and a sacrifice,
A Holy Spirit's energies,
An advocate with God.

These, these prepare us for the sight
Of Holiness above:
The sons of ignorance and night
May dwell in the eternal light
Through the eternal love!

—*Thomas Binney*

Isaiah recorded his experience: "In the year that King Uzziah died I saw the Lord sitting upon a throne . . ." (Isa. 6:1). What did Isaiah see? He could not have seen God and lived, but he saw some manifestation of the glory of God. Some believe it was a Christophany (an appearance of Christ in the Old Testament). In the light of this vision of glory, the seraphim bowed in extreme reverence and cried, "Holy, Holy, Holy is the LORD of hosts. . . ." Isaiah's response was utterly appropriate; "Woe is me! . . . for I am a man of unclean lips . . ." (vv. 1-5). Paul seems to refer to this glory: "And then the lawless one will be revealed, and the Lord Jesus will slay him with the breath of his mouth and destroy him by his appearing and his coming" (2 Thess. 2:8). This is a revealing and inspiring passage, but the latter part is more significant: ". . . will destroy him by his appearance." Can a mere appearance destroy? The New English Bible translation is even more graphic: ". . . that wicked man whom the Lord Jesus will destroy with the breath of his mouth, and annihilate by the radiance of his coming" (2 Thess. 2:9). Here is graphic and startling evidence that impurity and evil will be scorched and destroyed by the sheer radiance of God's holiness and glory. Just as flesh and blood can be dissolved when it comes into contact with the concentrated light of a laser beam, so it is not hard to imagine what would happen if a man were brought before the unveiled glory of God. No wonder the Scripture says that "our God is a consuming fire." This unimpaired holiness is an attribute of the Trinity. Jesus is holy, God the Father is holy, and, as His name emphasizes, the Holy Spirit is holiness personified. What a thought that this Spirit of holiness and glory lives in our lives! No wonder Paul told his readers to "glorify God in your body." The very name Holy Spirit is suggestive. It certainly does not mean that the Spirit is more holy than the Father and the Son; perhaps He is called Holy because He works on earth and in the personality of Christians. It is important to stress that He is not in the least inferior to the rest of the Godhead in holiness.

I have long had a conviction that if revival does come in our day it will not be by "Madison Avenue" methods. Rather, it will come when Christians have seen the glory and holiness of God and are, as a consequence, broken before God—as were Moses, Isaiah, Paul, and many others.

A. W. Tozer has written that the God of contemporary Christianity is only slightly superior to the gods of Greece and Rome,[1] thus indicating how feeble our view of God is.

---

[1]Tozer, *The Knowledge of the Holy,* p. 16.

The Holy Spirit can never become more holy because He is already the absolute perfection of holiness.

THE OMNIPOTENCE OF THE HOLY SPIRIT

As we think about the omnipotence of the Holy Spirit we stress the fact that there is no limit to His power. In the past five years man has had to face the fact that there are limits to the supplies of energy he needs, whether they be power from mineral sources, or even solar energy. This was unthinkable twenty years ago. In the face of this we emphasize the point that in the Holy Spirit there is limitless power. At a time when man admits the limits to his power, what a wonderful time to stress the limitless power of God.

There needs to be a word of caution; the Holy Spirit cannot do anything that is a contradiction in itself. He cannot make three fives become thirty-five. He cannot make a stone that He cannot lift. These are logical impossibilities, not signs of limitations on His part.

Well can we say with the Old Testament writer, "Thine, O LORD, *is the greatness, and the power,* and the glory, and the victory, and the majesty; for all that is in the heavens and in the earth is thine; thine is the kingdom, O LORD, and thou art exalted as head above all. Both riches and honor come from thee, and thou rulest over all. In thy hand are *power and might; and in thy hand it is to make great and to give strength to all.* And now we thank thee, our God, and praise thy glorious name" (1 Chron. 29:11-13, italics mine).

It is a thought alien to man that God spends no energy that must be replenished. Modern science does not support the view that the world is self-sufficient; the second law of thermodynamics states the world is in a state of decline. To be sure, we do not know when this decline will have reached its ultimate limit, but it contrasts with the energies of God, who is self-sufficient. God's limitless power means that He is dependent upon nothing and no one. He has chosen to use us, but He does not need us.

As soon as a baby is born it begins to die. Cells die and are discarded but new ones take their place; the process continues until replacement is slower than wastage. God's power is never like that. "Once God has spoken; twice have I heard this: that power belongs to God" (Ps. 62:11). For David this was no overworked phrase that tripped lightly off the tongue. His whole life was based on that sure foundation.

Just as we cannot comprehend the ultimate of holiness, so we cannot grasp the concept of unlimited power. We think of nuclear power, and rightly dread to hear of first-strike capability and second-strike. We know something about the power that lasers and microwaves have to shatter rocks. God laughs at them all, for He alone is the source of all power. "The God who made the world and everything in it, being Lord of heaven and earth, does not live in shrines made by man, nor is he served by human hands, as though he needed anything, since he himself gives to all men life and breath and everything" (Acts 17:24-25). "The weakness of God is stronger than men" (1 Cor. 1:25).

Omnipotence and sovereignty go together, and this is true of the Godhead. He cannot be manipulated or coerced. As Paul discovered, God's power is perfected in human weakness. Again and again we find ourselves powerless until we recognize as a certainty that the Holy Spirit is within us, and that His power is limitless. Kings and emperors in their day have longed for unlimited power, and some have almost achieved it in a limited way, but there has always been one power that has eluded them. Rulers have had the power to take life (six million Jews perished in Hitler's gas chambers), but none had the power to give life. The Grecian king Alexander conquered all of the then-known world, but died a frustrated man at the age of 35. All Hitler's fantasies of a thousand-year Reich perished with his own body in a sordid bunker in East Berlin.

Only the Holy Spirit has the power to give life that cannot be measured or destroyed. Paul wrote, "I am not ashamed of the gospel; it is the power of God for salvation" (Rom 1:16). He was addressing Christians who lived in the most powerful empire in the world. In the quaint English village of Fletching, Sussex, there is a small but beautiful church. In it is buried the body of Gibbon who wrote *The Decline and Fall of the Roman Empire,* the monumental work which is a fitting epitaph to what had been one of the greatest empires in the world. The power of the Roman Empire could take Paul's life, but not before a group of Christians had been established in Caesar's household.

> Crowns and thrones may perish,
> Kingdoms rise and wane,
> But the church of Jesus
> Constant will remain.
> —Sabine Baring-Gould

Because of the limitless power of the Holy Spirit, the waves of time and persecution have lashed in vain against the true church of Christ. Job said, "I know that thou canst do all things, and that no purpose of thine can be thwarted" (Job 42:2). These are words to cheer the struggling soul, especially if we link them with Paul's reminder: "We know that in everything God works for good with those who love him . . ." (Rom. 8:28). Nothing, not man's evil cunning or even our own stupidity, can frustrate the will of God in our lives.

THE HOLY SPIRIT AND LOVE

Raw, limitless power can be a fearsome thing to face. "Power corrupts, and absolute power corrupts absolutely." There is much to this old expression, but we are dealing with power in the Person who is absolute holiness, so corruption is out of the question here. We come to another characteristic of the Holy Spirit, and that is our safeguard. He is not only limitless power, but also *limitless love.* "That you, being rooted and grounded in love, may have power to comprehend . . . what is the breadth and length and height and depth, and to know the love of Christ which surpasses knowledge" (Eph. 3:17-19). "God is love" (1 John 4:8).

Just as Paul and others almost competed to express the wonder of the love of God, and found that language is inadequate, so also the poets and hymn writers have almost surpassed themselves in this exercise. John Greenleaf Whittier, the Massachusetts Quaker, put it thus:

> Immortal Love—forever full,
> Forever flowing free,
> Forever shared, forever whole,
> A never-ebbing sea!

Whittier, struggling to describe the love of God, compares it with a mighty sea that is forever flowing, forever shared by others but never diminished. Nothing can exhaust it, but not merely so; nothing can even cause an ebb tide! With God, love is always at high tide. This image has been used again and again. Samuel Trevor Francis expresses it in his hymn:

> O the deep, deep love of Jesus—
> Vast, unmeasured, boundless, free!
> Rolling as a mighty ocean
> In its fullness over me.
> Underneath me, all around me,
> Is the current of Thy love—
> Leading onward, leading homeward,
> To my glorious rest above.

Love is a word debased by common usage; God's love is a holy love, without moods. It is a constant and unvarying force, not a fitful emotion. The prophet Zephaniah was speaking of reality, not theory, when he wrote, "The LORD, your God, is in your midst, a warrior who gives victory; he will rejoice over you with gladness, he will renew you in his love" (Zeph. 3:17).

> O give thanks to the LORD, for he is good;
>   for his steadfast love endures for ever!
> Let them thank the LORD for his steadfast love,
>   for his wonderful works to the sons of men!
> (Ps. 107:1,8)

The Attributes of the Holy Spirit

Our Lord said, "Greater love has no man than this, that a man lay down his life for his friends" (John 15:13). It is wonderful that the Holy Spirit is the One who has all knowledge, including that of ourselves and our sin; but He is also perfect love and loves us despite what we are.

THE UNLIMITED PRESENCE OF THE HOLY SPIRIT

We have become used to thinking of our age as the "space age." It is startling to recognize that thousands of years ago King David was frequently thinking and writing about space, both at night and during the day. He was a military man of heroic dimensions, but he also knew the agony of betrayal, loneliness, and fear. Despite these experiences he could write, "Such knowledge is too wonderful for me; it is high, I cannot attain it. Whither shall I go from thy Spirit? Or whither shall I flee from thy presence? If I ascend to heaven, thou art there! If I made my bed in Sheol, thou art there! If I take the wings of the morning and dwell in the uttermost parts of the sea, even there thy hand shall lead me, and thy right hand shall hold me. If I say, 'Let only darkness cover me, and the light about me be night,' even the darkness is not dark to thee, the night is bright as the day; for darkness is as light with thee" (Ps. 139:6-12).

It is not merely true that the Spirit is everywhere; He *is* the everywhere. David was not alone in drawing comfort from the vastness of the Lord. Paul exclaims exuberantly, "Who shall separate us from the love of Christ? Shall tribulation, or distress, or persecution, or famine, or nakedness, or peril, or sword?. . . No, in all these things we are more than conquerors through him who loved us. For I am sure that neither death, nor life, nor angels, nor principalities, nor things present, nor things to come, nor powers, nor height, nor depth, nor anything else in all creation, will be able to separate us from the love of God in Christ Jesus our Lord" (Rom. 8:35-39).

David's son Solomon grasped this thought, and expressed it at the dedication of the Temple he had built: "Behold, heaven and the highest heaven cannot contain thee" (1 Kings 8:27).

The dictionary defines infinity as "anything infinite, endless, or unlimited space, time, distance, quantity, etc." This can be a terrifying thought as depicted by the French existentialist Jean-Paul Sartre in his play *No Exit*. When applied to God, however, it refers not merely to quantity but also to quality. The Bible abounds with references to the limitless presence of God, but generally in a way that comforts rather than threatens.

Francis Thompson was once a man on the run from God, and in his poem *The Hound of Heaven* he describes the wonderful blessing of being eventually captured by God and His love. It is popularly claimed in many circles that it is presumptuous to speak of the things of God as certainties, and that man is not more than a seeker after truth. The Bible has no time for such nonsense, and makes it clear that He who inhabits eternity is also the one who inhabits the human heart. He is at the same time far away and closer than our own hands and feet. This thought is well expressed in the words of the following hymn:

> Lord of all being throned afar,
> Thy glory flames from sun and star.
> Center and soul of every sphere
> Yet to each loving heart how near.
> —*Oliver Wendell Homes*

There is no place or situation in which we can find ourselves, but that God is with us. The only separation from God that man can know is the separation caused by disobedience to Him. God ordained that man should be a dependent being in close relationship with Himself. When man rebels and violates that divine order, he also violates that relationship.

In the words of A. W. Tozer, "Thereafter he (man) became not a planet revolving around the central sun but a sun around which everything else must revolve." God does not accept man's terms for His nearness but rather is the sun around which we revolve and from whom we take our comfort and enjoy fellowship.

The Attributes of the Holy Spirit

FOR DISCUSSION

1. What is the "unforgivable sin"?
2. Do we often hear or read about the attributes of God?
3. Is every attribute of God an attribute of the Holy Spirit?
4. What is an attribute?
5. Name at least five attributes of the Holy Spirit.
6. The Bible does not commend human ignorance or human knowledge. Why is this?
7. Give references where the Bible stresses the unlimited knowledge of the Holy Spirit.
8. Does the Holy Spirit accumulate knowledge?
9. Name some of the occasions when the apostle John saw glimpses of the glory and holiness of God.
10. Can man look upon God?
11. How can a person become holy?
12. What is the meaning of "omnipotence"?
13. Does the power of God need to be replenished?
14. Where did the psalmist David write about the presence of God?

5

The Holy Spirit
and the Old Testament

Not all the activity of the Holy Spirit in the Old Testament period is documented, but there are more references to Him and His work than seems to be generally recognized. J. E. Elder Cumming in his book, *Through the Eternal Spirit,* Stirling Tract Enterprise, London, lists eighty-eight passages in the Old Testament in which the Holy Spirit is directly mentioned, and that is a conservative number.

It is difficult, and perhaps even impossible, to have an accurate grasp of the person and work of the Holy Spirit in the New Testament unless we can see the contrast to the way He worked in the Old Testament. In ministry concerning the Holy Spirit today it is common almost to ignore the Old Testament, except for an occasional reference to the prophecy of Joel. It is dangerous to leap straight from His work at the beginning of Genesis, hovering over chaos and bringing forth the order and beauty of creation, to His work at Pentecost and after.

The Old Testament speaks of the Holy Spirit in three tenses.

1. It refers to the work of the Holy Spirit in the past, such as creation.
2. It narrates what He is doing with an individual in the present tense, as when it tells of His coming upon David.
3. It records prophecies of what the Holy Spirit will do in the future, such as Joel's prophecy that there would be an outpouring of the Spirit after the work of the Atonement (Joel 2:28-29). In his work *The Holy Spirit,* published by Banner of Truth, George Smeaton

poses the question whether Adam before the Fall had the Holy Spirit. He asserts definitely that he had, and cites Romans 5:12-14 as evidence, and goes on to stress that the Spirit was withdrawn from Adam after the Fall.

There seems to be at least six notable characteristics of the work of the Holy Spirit in the Old Testament. It would be well to look at them in some detail, although this is not the place to examine every reference to the Holy Spirit in the Old Testament. It will not be easy to fully grasp our subject without first dealing with the six following principles:

1. The Holy Spirit was given only to a relatively few selected individuals.
2. He was usually given to enable rather than to accomplish some specific ministry.
3. He had little effect upon their personal moral characters.
4. His presence in a person could be withdrawn.
5. His continued presence in a person depended upon obedience from that person.
6. His coming upon a person was different from the making of them into "the temple of the Holy Spirit" which occurred after Pentecost.

The terminology of the Holy Spirit's work in the Old Testament varies; sometimes this seems significant and at other times less so. It is interesting to note that there are only two cases where it is stated that the Holy Spirit dwelt in a man. The first is Joseph: "Can we find such a man as this, *in whom is the Spirit of God?*" (Gen. 41:38, italics mine). It is unlikely that Pharaoh understood the full significance of what he said, but the life of Joseph would suggest that it was perfectly accurate. The second man of whom this is said is Joshua. When a leader was being sought who could be a worthy successor to Moses, the Lord said to Moses, "Take Joshua the son of Nun, *a man in whom is the spirit,* and lay your hand upon him" (Num. 27:18, italics mine). We read of Moses not that the Holy Spirit was in him, but that "the LORD came down in the cloud and spoke to him, and took some of the spirit that was upon him and put it upon the seventy elders; and when the spirit rested upon them, they prophesied. But they did so no more" (Num. 11:25). So we read that in the case of Joseph and Joshua the Spirit was "in them," but in the case of Moses the Spirit was "upon him." Bearing in mind the unique place that Moses has in the history of the Israelites, his constant concern for the glory of God, and the radiance that shone from his face after communion with God, it would be rash indeed to give him an inferior position to that of Joseph and Joshua. Thus there would seem to be little significant difference in the use of these two terms.

There are a number of instances of the Holy Spirit working through men in the Book of Judges, but for our purposes we shall see certain principles revealed in the life of one person, Samson. In Judges 13:25 we read that "The *Spirit of the LORD began to stir him* (italics mine) in Mahaneh-dan, between Zorah and Eshta-ol." In Judges 14:5-6 we read, "And behold, a young lion roared against him; and the Spirit of the LORD came mightily upon him, and he tore the lion asunder as one tears a kid." Again, "The Spirit of the LORD came mightily upon him, and he went down to Ashkelon and killed thirty men of the town" (v. 19). Then later on we read that "the Spirit of the LORD came mightily upon him, and the ropes which were on his arms became as flax that has caught fire, and his bonds melted off his hands. And he found a fresh jawbone of an ass, and put out his hand and seized it, and with it he slew a thousand men" (Judges 15:14-15).

We are told that "he judged Israel in the days of the Philistines twenty years" (v. 20). We have not by any means been given every detail of his superhuman physical strength, but we have enough to show that it was connected with the Holy Spirit who came upon him. To see the explanation of all this we turn to Judges 13:2-5. "And there was a certain man of Zorah, of the tribe of the Danites, whose name was Manoah; and his wife was barren and had no children. And the angel of the LORD appeared to the woman and said to her, 'Behold, you are barren and have no children; but you shall conceive and bear a son. Therefore beware, and drink no wine or strong drink, and eat nothing unclean, for lo, you shall conceive and bear a son. No razor shall come upon his head, for the boy shall be a Nazirite to God from birth; and he shall begin to deliver Israel from the hand of the Philistines.'" The whole story of his life is contained in the following four chapters. Despite the presence of the Holy Spirit, his morals were loose and he repeatedly consorted with harlots. One condition of the Nazirite vow was that his hair was not to be cut. That Samson was aware of the source of his strength and how far he could lose it, is clear from what he told Delilah. The fact that he permitted Delilah to have his hair cut off was an act of disobedience. We read that "he told her all his mind, and said to her, 'A razor has never come upon my head; for I have been a Nazirite to God from my mother's womb. If I be shaved, then my strength will leave me, and I shall become weak, and be like any other man'" (Judges 16:17). The last tragic sentence, "And he did not know that the LORD had left him" (v. 20), is significant for two reasons. First, it indicates that the Lord had been with him on a continuing basis, and second, that the Lord left him after his act of disobedience.

Some similar lessons are stressed again in the experience of Saul and David. The Israelites refused to listen to the voice of Samuel the prophet and insisted upon having a king. Israel was not a people ruled by themselves, a democracy, but a people governed by God, a theocracy. God eventually assented to their pleading, however, and gave instructions to Samuel to appoint Saul as king. "Now the day before Saul came, the LORD had revealed to Samuel: 'Tomorrow about this time I will send to you a man from the land of Benjamin, and you shall anoint him to be prince over my people Israel. He shall save my people from the hand of the Philistines; for I have seen the affliction of my people, because their cry has come to me.' Then Samuel took a vial of oil and poured it on his head, and kissed him and said, 'Has not the LORD anointed you to be prince over his people Israel? And you shall reign over the people of the LORD and you will save them from the hand of their enemies round about. And this shall be the sign to you that the LORD has anointed you to be prince over his heritage..."' (1 Sam. 9:15-16; 10:1). We further read in 1 Samuel 10:9-10 that when "he turned his back to leave Samuel, God gave him another heart; and all these signs came to pass that day. When they came to Gibeah, behold, a band of prophets met him; and the spirit of God came mightily upon him, and he prophesied among them." Later on we read that "the spirit of God came mightily upon Saul when he heard these words..." (1 Sam. 11:6). Then follows a graphic description of a decisive victory over the Ammonites followed by the coronation of Saul as king. First Samuel chapters 9-31 describe his reign. It is a pathetic story of man of great courage who was eventually rejected by God because of disobedience, who became eaten up by jealousy and melancholy, and eventually died by suicide on the battlefield (1 Sam. 31:4).

For the purpose of this study, 1 Samuel 16 has a special significance. Verse 1 reveals how God told Samuel that Saul had been rejected and another was to be anointed. Verse 12 reveals that the man chosen to be the next king was David, and verses 13-14 read: "Then Samuel took the horn of oil, and anointed him in the midst of his brothers; and the Spirit of the LORD came mightily upon David from that day forward. And Samuel rose up, and went to Ramah. Now the Spirit of the LORD departed from Saul, and an evil spirit from the LORD tormented him." These two verses, revealing the Spirit of the Lord coming upon David and departing from Saul, must rank as one of the saddest incidents in the Old Testament. We must look at some of their implications.

The narrative makes it clear that the Holy Spirit was with Samson, Saul, and David on a continuing basis. In the cases of both Samson and Saul we read of the Spirit leaving them after their disobedience. Saul continued to reign for many years, but spiritually he was a desolate and forlorn figure—an empty shell.

These three all had great experiences with the Holy Spirit, but it is essential to recognize the fact that their experiences were quite unlike the experiences of believers after Pentecost. In the Old Testament there is no record of the Holy Spirit as a sanctifier, which partly explains the moral behavior of these men. As René Pache has pointed out, it is nowhere stated in the Old Testament that every Israelite received the Holy Spirit.[1] In no way can these men have had the experience of being "temples of the Holy Spirit," as it is stated in John 7:39, "For as yet the Spirit had not been given, because Jesus was not yet glorified." We today are living in the age of the Holy Spirit. Later we shall look more closely at some of the implications of this. However, this reference in John 7 (and many others) makes it clear that before the Holy Spirit could be poured out, and all God's children become dwelling places of the Holy Spirit, there had to be the cleansing and atoning work of Jesus Christ.

It may well be asked why David did not have the Spirit withdrawn like Samson and Saul, when at times his conduct descended to adultery and murder. That David recognized this as a possibility is obvious from his wonderful psalm of repentance, Psalm 51. He never forgot what he had seen happen in the life of Saul years before. When rebuked for his sin by Nathan the prophet in 2 Samuel 12, his response was immediate: "David said to Nathan, 'I have sinned against the LORD'" (v. 13). It was after this experience that he wrote Psalm 51. It is important to read this psalm, to take time to absorb its truth, and to recognize David's humility and sorrow, for it is the key to his life. Particularly note verses 10-11: "Create in me a clean heart, O God, and put a new and right spirit within me. Cast me not away from thy presence, and *take not thy holy Spirit from me*" (italics mine). After seeing Saul's experience, it was no wonder that what David dreaded most was to be deserted by God, to have the Holy Spirit withdrawn.

What distinguished David from Samson and Saul was his repeated repentance when he sinned. This sensitivity was certainly one of the qualities that caused him to be called a man

[1]René Pache, *The Person and Work of the Holy Spirit* (Chicago: Moody Press, 1954).

after God's own heart (Acts 13:22). The incident referred to in 2 Samuel 12 and Psalm 51 is not merely a single occurrence. The quality that set David apart was his sensivitity to sin and repentance for it. It is a quality seldom preached about today. It is true that if we are disobedient to God we shall lose the full blessing of fellowship with Him, but the Holy Spirit will not be withdrawn. The New Testament, and 1 John in particular, stresses that continual fellowship depends upon repentance of sin. This is only one of the many lessons we can learn from the life of David.

At the beginning of this chapter we noticed that the Old Testament revealed the work of the Holy Spirit in the past tense (e.g. creation), in the present tense (e.g. Samson and David), and in the future tense, when the prophets told of the work of the Holy Spirit that was to come.

The work of the prophets was not only foretelling the future but also forthtelling. In other words, they usually were men with a message from God to their own people. When we think of their foretelling of the future we often feel that they were concerned only or mainly with the fact that a Messiah was going to appear. Of course it is true that this was one of their main ministries, but this was by no means their only one. They also foretold the outpouring of the Holy Spirit, one of the greatest blessings that the Christ would make possible.

In Ezekiel 11:5 we read that *"the Spirit of the LORD fell upon me,* and he said to me, 'Say, Thus says the Lord . . .' " (italics mine). In verses 19-20 God promised that "I will give them one heart, *and put a new spirit within them;* I will take the stony heart out of their flesh and give them a heart of flesh, that they may walk in my statutes and keep my ordinances and obey them; and they shall be my people, and I will be their God" (italics mine).

Again and again we read that the prophecies of the Old Testament were inspired by the Holy Spirit. "And when he spoke to me, *the Spirit entered into me and set me upon my feet"* (Ezek. 2:2, italics mine). The promise in Ezekiel 11:19-20 includes the fact that God will give a new spirit and a new heart, and the power to walk in obedience to Himself.

56

There are many other prophecies such as, "And he will come to Zion as Redeemer, to those in Jacob who turn from transgression, says the LORD. And as for me, this is my covenant with them, says the LORD: *my spirit which is upon you,* and my words which I have put in your mouth, shall not depart out of your mouth, or out of the mouth of your children, or out of the mouth of your children's children, says the LORD, from this time forth and for evermore" (Isa. 59:20-21, italics mine).

The clearest passage is in Joel 2:28-32: "And it shall come to pass afterward, that I will pour out my spirit on all flesh; your sons and your daughters shall prophesy, your old men shall dream dreams, and your young men shall see visions. Even upon the menservants and maidservants in those days, I will pour out my spirit. And I will give portents in the heavens and on the earth, blood and fire and columns of smoke. The sun shall be turned to darkness, and the moon to blood, before the great and terrible day of the Lord comes. And it shall come to pass that all who call upon the name of the LORD shall be delivered; for in Mount Zion and in Jerusalem there shall be those who escape, as the LORD has said, and among the survivors shall be those whom the LORD calls."

What makes this passage the most significant one concerning the Holy Spirit in the Old Testament is that when the Holy Spirit was poured out at Pentecost, Peter immediately linked it with Joel's prophecy. ". . . this is what was spoken by the prophet Joel: 'And in the last days it shall be, God declares, that I will pour out my Spirit upon all flesh, and your sons and your daughters shall prophesy, and your young men shall see visions, and your old men shall dream dreams'" (Acts 2:16-17).

It is not clear that this prophecy meant very much to the people to whom Joel was directly addressing himself. However, the function of prophecy is not merely to inform us of future events; it also enables us, when an event takes place, to do as Peter did. We can look to what God said in the past and say to people who are confused and needy, "This is what God promised many years ago."

Joel was promising that the Holy Spirit would work in men

and women in a way in which He did not work in the Old Testament. Following are four examples:

1. "I will pour out my Spirit on all flesh." In the days of the Old Testament the Holy Spirit was given only to individuals of one race, the Israelites. The prophecy mentions that in this new movement He will be poured out upon all flesh. Even Peter did not recognize the full implication of this. In the Acts of the Apostles we learn that God took real pains to convince him that the Holy Spirit was for the Gentiles as well as the Jews (Acts 10).

2. We noticed at the beginning of this chapter that even among the Israelites only a few selected people were given the Holy Spirit; usually for some special ministry, such as leadership or prophecy. In Joel the Holy Spirit is promised to "your sons and daughters, the old and the young." This speaks of a work among the whole people of God. It means the possibility of a whole church inhabited by the Spirit in a way impossible in the Old Testament.

3. To stress that these will not be in any way extraordinary people God says that "even upon the menservants and maidservants in those days, I will pour out my Spirit."

4. He promises that "it shall be that whoever calls on the name of the Lord shall be saved." In Acts 2:41 we read that on that single occasion those who received the word and responded numbered 3,000 people.

Much more teaching concerning the Holy Spirit is to be found in the gospels and the rest of the New Testament, but the great and unusual outpouring was something that God had promised before and thus Peter was able to look back and say in effect, "God keeps His word." He is a covenant-keeping God. In Peter's sermon at Pentecost he stressed the fact that this could not have taken place without our Lord's death and resurrection. "This Jesus God raised up, and of that we all are witnesses. Being therefore exalted at the right hand of God, and having received from the Father the promise of the Holy Spirit, he has poured out this which you see and hear" (Acts 2:32-33). After his sermon they were "cut to the heart" with conviction of sin and asked "What shall we do?" (v. 37). Peter's reply is significant. "Repent, and be baptized every one of you in the name of Jesus Christ for the forgiveness of your sins; *and you shall receive the gift of the Holy Spirit*" (vv. 37-38, italics mine). No one had been able to say this before in the whole of the Old Testament.

Now we have seen a little of the work and the promise of the Holy Spirit from the beginning to the end of the Old Testament. Let us take comfort that the promise is to us whether we are near or "far off."

FOR DISCUSSION

1. In what tenses does the Old Testament speak of the Holy Spirit?

2. Give at least four principles of the work of the Holy Spirit in the Old Testament.

3. There are only two men in the Old Testament of whom it is written "in whom the Spirit is." Who are they?

4. What condition was Samson to keep in order to keep the presence of the holy spirit?

5. What is the difference between a democracy and a theocracy?

6. Why did the Holy Spirit depart from King Saul?

7. Samson, Saul, and David all had great experiences of the Holy Spirit in their lives. Were they similar to the experiences of believers after Pentecost?

8. Why was the Holy Spirit withdrawn from Saul after he had sinned? Why was the Holy Spirit not withdrawn from David after he sinned?

9. Where do we find evidence of David's repentance?

10. The prophet Joel prophesied that the Holy Spirit would be poured out. Give three ways in which this experience was to differ from the work of the Holy Spirit in the Old Testament.

6

The Holy Spirit and Common Grace

When I pulled aside the tinseled layers of commercialism obscuring the true significance of Christmas, my mind boggled at the thought that the God of glory could, in the person of the Christ child, have resided temporarily in the dark filthiness of a Middle Eastern stable.

As time passed by it became eclipsed in my mind by an even more wonderful truth: that the same holy God of light, in whom there is no shadow, would live permanently in the soiled and sinful personalities of those who invite Him into their lives. "Do you not know that your body is a temple of the Holy Spirit. . . ? You are not your own; for you were bought with a price. So glorify God in your body" (1 Cor. 6:19-20). This is no new truth, but it is certainly a neglected one. It is a truth bursting with glorious possibilities, but one not without problems. For example, how can God the Holy Spirit, whose power is limitless, inhabit the puny body of a human baby? How can the Spirit which is *holy* be found in a body that is depraved? How can One who is unlimited truth live within the confines of a frail human intellect?

The episode of the stable may cast some rays of light on these matters. God the Son, as Jesus Christ the baby, had limitless knowledge, but as a baby He had no power of speech to express that knowledge. Geoffrey Bull, in writing so perceptively of his three years in a Red Chinese prison, puts it this way:

Many an hour I would traverse my little space. No one knows save those who have the strange experience just what it means

60

to be shut indefinitely in a small dark place alone. This sense of enclosure is nevertheless still relative. I would think of the insects. They could be where I was, with no sense of restraint. They could creep the walls and know no claustrophobia. . . . What must it then have been for Him? The uncontained in all the heaven of the heavens, couched in a baby boy beneath the stable thatch.[1]

Few Christians would question the need for a tidal wave of the Holy Spirit in the church of Christ today. Few, however, seem to know where to begin or how to understand Him. Twenty years ago the Holy Spirit was hidden by neglect; today He is hidden by excess.

If we are to experience the abundance of God's power in our lives, the first things we must ask in these pages are: Who is He who lives within the person of the Christian, and what is He like? What is His role in me? What is His role in time and eternity?

I have said that first my mind boggled at the thought of the God-child in a stable, and that later it seemed an even greater wonder that God the Holy Spirit is willing to live in a fallen personality. There is a further marvel I mention with awe and reverence, for I understand it so imperfectly. It is the thought that He not merely condescends to live in us, but allows us in large measure to restrict or to release the degree of liberty He has in our lives. To me is given the awesome power to "quench the Spirit" (1 Thess. 5:19), to "grieve the Spirit" (Eph. 4:30), or yet to "be filled with the Spirit" (Eph. 5:18). This truth is not merely an enormous responsibility for us, but is conclusive evidence that God does not selfishly grasp His rightful privilege nor suffer from the merest shadow of insecurity. He delegates to man the right to decide His degree of fullness in every person.

Many Christians talk as if the Holy Spirit came into existence at Pentecost, but we have seen that he is mentioned from the

[1]Geoffrey T. Bull, *God Holds the Key* (Chicago: Moody Press, 1959).

61

beginning, in fact in the first chapter of the Bible. Still more Christians make the mistake of thinking that He is not active today, except in the lives of those regenerate people who have accepted Christ as their Savior. It is true that natural man is dead to the things of God, that his eyes of understanding for spiritual things have been closed. To use another expression, he is depraved. We must be clear what this means. James Packer has defined human depravity as follows: "It means that man is not in every point as bad as he could be, but in no point is he as good as he should be."

Even in unregenerate depraved man the Holy Spirit is still at work. He is not at work in a saving way, but He is at work in a restraining way. This is called *common grace*. Edwin Palmer has explained that "it is *grace* because it is undeserved. . . . it is *common* because it is regarded as not only for the elect, but for the non-elect too."[2] This in no way makes a man righteous in the sight of God, but His restraining power is at work in the lives of non-Christians. Life in the world is tolerable only because God exercises this restraining power. If, or when, this power is withdrawn and the venom of sin that is in the blood of all men remains unchecked, the result will be so loathsome that the human mind cannot imagine it. Stephen said to the Jews in Acts 7:51 that "you always resist the Holy Spirit." This implies that the Spirit had worked in them.

We must be grateful to God that this is so, for life would be intolerable if it weren't. When the Antichrist is ruling unchecked, the times and situations will be terrible, beyond imagination.

Many non-Christians today perform acts that in themselves may seem in harmony with Christian practice; they care for the aged, they give money for good causes. None of these things can bring salvation in the slightest degree, but they are still prompted by the Holy Spirit. The fact that man does not give credit to the Holy Spirit, but mistakenly believes that it may

---

[2]Edwin Palmer, *The Person and Ministry of the Holy Spirit* (Grand Rapids: Baker Book House, 1974).

bring him credit in the eyes of God, in no way changes the fact that this is part of the work of the Holy Spirit in common grace.

FOR DISCUSSION

1. What is the temple of the Holy Spirit?
2. What causes the Holy Spirit to be hidden?
3. Do we have power to limit the working of the Holy Spirit? Give reasons for your conclusion.
4. Is the Holy Spirit at work today outside the life of believers?
5. What is meant by the Holy Spirit and common grace?

7

The Holy Spirit in the Gospels

It is natural to think of the division between the Old Testament and the New as being a dividing line in the progress of God's purpose, but Pentecost is in fact that division. It is at that point that God's dealings with man entered a new dimension, and great new possibilities opened to those who heeded and responded to the call of God. In most respects God's dealings with men in the gospels are similar to His dealings in the Old Testament.

The case of John the Baptist is an important illustration. John was in prison, his information about Jesus Christ and His activities would have been fragmentary, and probably John was puzzled and depressed. His disciples came to Jesus and asked, "Are you he who is to come, or shall we look for another?" And Jesus answered them, "Go and tell John what you hear and see: the blind receive their sight and the lame walk, lepers are cleansed and the deaf hear, and the dead are raised up, and the poor have good news preached to them. And blessed is he who takes no offense at me" (Matt. 11:2-6). Jesus continued to talk about John and made a statement that was at once an enormous compliment and a great enigma. The compliment: "Truly, I say to you, among those born of woman there has risen no one greater than John the Baptist." The enigma: "Yet he who is least in the kingdom of heaven is greater than he" (v. 11).

There had been a gap of 400 years between the last of the Old Testament prophets and John's appearance on the scene. When he did begin to preach his message it was a mixture of denunciation of sin and the news that the Messiah was at hand. John was the last and the greatest of the prophets of the old covenant. "Yet he who is least in the kindgom of heaven is greater than he." What did John lack that obscure believers would enjoy? He was destined for martyrdom and would never live to see the atoning death of Christ, the triumph of the Resurrection, and Pentecost. Jesus said later in His ministry that "the law and the prophets were until John; since then the good news of the kingdom of God is preached, and every one enters it violently" (Luke 16:16).

While the gospels are related to the Old Testament, they in .fact cover a relatively brief period of approximately thirty years. More space is devoted to covering that time span than any similar period in the Bible. The events that took place during that time are so important that they are put under a microscope and magnified so we will not miss their significance. Thus the period of the gospels is essentially one of transition. In studying it we shall see that in every step the Holy Spirit has a very important place, from the beginning to the end.

THE INCARNATION

In the gospels supreme prominence is naturally given to the person of Jesus Christ, so that some have even gone so far as to suggest that if Christ is really God the work of the Holy Spirit is unnecessary. To make such a division within the Trinity is of course not only unscriptural, it is heresy. John Owen states concerning the work of the three members of the Trinity that "there is no such division in the external operation of God that any one of them should be the act of one person, without concurrence of the other." The Incarnation was and remains a great mystery, but this is purely because of our limited understanding. Controversy still rages about it and many theologians prefer to believe that it is a symbolic rather than a literal fact. Such a view is incompatible with the biblical account. Curiosity as to the precise form of the Incarnation has been common from the virgin mother herself until our own day. Curiosity and puzzlement are one thing, unbelief quite another.

The Incarnation was a voluntary act of God the Son as is clear from Philippians 2:7: "[He] emptied himself, taking the form of a servant, being born in the likeness of men." Phillips' paraphrase makes the meaning clearer: "For he, who had always been God by nature, did not cling to his privileges as God's equal, but stripped himself of every advantage by consenting to be a slave by nature and being born a man." It was also an act of God the Father. Consequently, when Christ came into the world, he said, " . . . a body hast thou prepared for me" (Heb. 10:5). That the Holy Spirit was active in the process of incarnation is clear from a number of Scripture passages. "Now the birth of Jesus Christ took place in this way. When his mother Mary had been betrothed to Joseph, before they came together she was found to be *with child of the Holy Spirit*" (Matt. 1:18, italics mine). In Jewish custom the betrothal lasted for one year, and although it did not permit normal marriage relations, it had great force in Jewish law and could be ended only by divorce. As Joseph planned a quiet divorce, "an angel of the Lord appeared to him in a dream, saying, 'Joseph, son of David, do not fear to take Mary your wife, for that which is conceived in her *is of the Holy Spirit*" (Matt. 1:20, italics mine).

The account in Luke 1 is more detailed: "In the sixth month the angel Gabriel was sent from God to a city of Galilee named Nazareth, to a virgin betrothed to a man whose name was Joseph, of the house of David; and the virgin's name was Mary. And he came to her and said, 'Hail, O favored one, the Lord is with you!' But she was greatly troubled at the saying, and considered in her mind what sort of greeting this might be. And the angel said to her, 'Do not be afraid, Mary, for you have found favor with God. And behold, you will conceive in your womb and bear a son, and you shall call his name Jesus. He will be great, and will be called the Son of the Most High; and the Lord God will give to him the throne of his father David, and he will reign over the house of Jacob for ever; and of his kingdom there will be no end.' And Mary said to the angel, 'How shall this be, since I have no husband?' And the angel said to her, '*The Holy Spirit will come upon you* (italics mine), and the power of the Most High will overshadow you; therefore the child to be born will be called holy, the Son of God'" (Luke 1:26-35). Note Mary's reaction to the news: "How shall this be, since I have no husband?" and the response: "The Holy Spirit will come upon you; and the power of the Most High will overshadow you; therefore the child to be born will be called holy, the Son of God."

Mary was not the last to be puzzled. The doctrine of the Incarnation has been a battleground for centuries. Failure to believe in the virgin birth has led to the dividing of denominations and the forming of new ones. The most far-fetched attempt to explain how the Savior could be born of a human being and still be the Son of God led the Roman Catholic church to the doctrine of the Immaculate Conception of the virgin Mary. Little notice need be taken of this apart from remarking that it is totally without foundation in the bible, and that if it were followed to its rational conclusion it might be possible to believe in the deity of Christ, but impossible to believe that He was also perfectly man. We have already seen that the Holy Spirit was involved in the creation of man, and now we see that He was the agent in the creation of Immanuel, "God with us." "God sent forth his Son, born of woman, born under the law" (Gal. 4:4).

Evangelicals have been accused of placing so much emphasis on the deity of Christ that they neglect His humanity. This criticism is a valid one. A strong emphasis on Christ's deity is important, however. Indeed, in assessing any religious teaching the first thing to ask is, "What is your opinion of Christ?" This is usually the acid test of any teaching. Because the deity of Christ has so often been attacked by heretics and theologians of the liberal school it is right that we continue to give great prominence to the doctrine, but not at the expense of teaching His humanity. If Christ had not taken upon Himself our humanity He could not have taken upon Himself our sin and therefore could not have provided the atonement for us; nor could we have had such close fellowship with Him. He was perfectly man, but He was sinless man, the only such man who ever lived.

Before leaving the subject it is essential to stress the fact that God the Son did not first come into existence at the time of the Incarnation. It is necessary to realize the fact of the preexistence of God the Son. Strictly speaking we should not use the name "Jesus" except for the period of time He spent on earth, for these words speak of His earthly ministry.

"And the child grew and became strong, filled with wisdom; and the favor of God was upon him" (Luke 2:40). This growth was an essential part of His humanity; perfection is quite compatible with growth. His deity knew no growth and needed none, but His humanity needed growth and it took place. When He was twelve years of age He was "sitting among the teachers, listening to them and asking them questions; and all who heard him were amazed at his understanding and his answers" (Luke 2:46-47). Jesus could reason with theologians at twelve years of age, but He could not have done so at two.

THE BAPTISM OF JESUS CHRIST

The next milestone in the life and ministry of our Lord was His baptism. We saw in chapter 2 that this was an occasion when all three members of the Trinity were manifested at once. "And when Jesus was baptized, he went up immediately from the water, and behold, the heavens were opened and he saw the Spirit of God descending like a dove, and alighting on him; and lo, a voice from heaven, saying, 'This is my beloved Son, with whom I am well pleased'" (Matt. 3:16-17). Much debate has surrounded this incident, particularly concerning the Holy Spirit descending like a dove. We are not to assume that before the time of Jesus' baptism He was without the aid and fellowship of the Holy Spirit, for from the moment of His conception there was perfect unity of all three members of the Trinity.

The baptism was His first public act; it marks the time when Jesus stepped out from the obscurity of His simple home at Nazareth into the spotlight of public ministry. It was the first time He was publicly authenticated by the Father.

There are a number of reasons why "the Spirit of God descended like a dove, and alighted on him." We have the words of John the Baptist: "I myself did not know him; but he who sent me to baptize with water said to me, 'He on whom you see the Spirit descend and remain, this is he who baptizes with the Holy Spirit.' And I have seen and have borne witness that this is the Son of God" (John 1:33-34). For John the visible symbol of the Holy Spirit descending upon Jesus Christ was evidently a previously promised sign, and evidence that He whom he had expected and publicly heralded was present and about to embark on His public ministry.

Nor was it a sign only for John. By its nature it was essentially an act that was public, a public sign of the Holy Spirit in Jesus. The voice from heaven was ample confirmation that the long-awaited Messiah of the Jews had arrived, but alas it made little or no impression upon them, "who received him not."

There was evidently a third reason. Although the Holy Spirit had been active in the earlier life of Jesus Christ, this was a special anointing for the active and public ministry that He was about to commence. In the narrative of the gospels the mention of the Holy Spirit in connection with Jesus Christ occurs and reoccurs. In Matthew, immediately following the occurrence of the voice from heaven, we read, "Then Jesus was led up *by the Spirit* into the wilderness to be tempted of the devil" (Matt. 4:1, italics mine). Luke's account is even more emphatic: "Jesus, *full of the Holy Spirit,* returned from the Jordan, and was *led by the Spirit* for forty days in the wilderness, tempted by the devil" (Luke 4:1-2, italics mine). In this confrontation between Jesus Christ and the devil, the initiative was taken by Jesus through the Holy Spirit; ever after in the life of Christ the devil was on the defensive.

This experience of temptation was followed by another significant event, recorded in Luke 4:14-21. The first significant thing is the phrase in verse 14, "And Jesus returned in the *power of the Spirit into Galilee*" (italics mine). This is followed by an event whose significance is not immediately obvious. In the Jewish synagogue, when the time came to read from the scrolls containing the prophets, it was customary for this honor to be delegated to a male visitor. My first experience of synagogue worship was during the Second World War. I clearly remember a young soldier in uniform home on leave, reading in Hebrew from the scroll. In the section beginning with verse 16 we learn that this task was entrusted to Jesus when He returned home to Nazareth and attended the synagogue. What is significant is the passage from which He read in Isaiah: "*The Spirit of the Lord GOD is upon me*, because the LORD has anointed me to bring good tidings to the afflicted; he has sent me to bind up the broken-hearted, to proclaim liberty to the captives, and the opening of the prison to those who are bound; to proclaim the year of the LORD's favor..." (Isa. 61:1-2, italics mine).

In Luke's record we read that He "closed the book, and gave it back to the attendant, and sat down; and the eyes of all in the synagogue were fixed on him" (Luke 4:20). Two things need to be noted. First, He stopped the reading in the middle of the quotation from Isaiah; second, He applied what He read to Himself: "Today this scripture has been fulfilled in your hearing" (Luke 4:21). He returned in the power of the Spirit to Galilee and stressed from Isaiah that "the Spirit of the Lord GOD is upon me." The quotation continues to outline the nature of the ministry upon which He was about to embark: "... to preach good news to the poor... to proclaim release to the captives, and recovering of sight to the blind, to set at liberty those who are oppressed, to proclaim the acceptable year of the Lord" (Luke 4:18-19).

It is remarkable that a prophecy uttered centuries before should have so complete a fulfillment, and especially that it associates that ministry with the Holy Spirit. Before we leave the passage, it is worth mentioning that when Jesus closed the book in the middle of the quotation, the part that He omitted to read was "and the day of vengeance of our God." He had come for deliverance but not for judgment.

Our Lord further attributes His public ministry to the power of the Holy Spirit when He says, "But if it is by the Spirit of God that I cast out demons, then the kingdom of God has come upon you" (Matt. 12:28). He goes on to stress in verse 32 that blasphemy against the Holy Spirit will not be forgiven. We need not look at all the implications of this statement, but one thing should be stressed. The whole context of this verse is a solemn warning that it is extremely dangerous to attribute the work of the Holy Spirit to the devil. In the earlier days of my Christian life, before the significance of this passage had occurred to me, I was quick to say of people who had experiences that were strange to me that they were of the devil. Now I am much more cautious. The ultimate blasphemy against the Holy Spirit is to deliberately reject His will to work in and through us.

I was once sharing the preaching at a Bible conference when one of the other speakers stated that "the gift of tongues was for national Israel in the first century and any such manifestation today is of the devil." In discussing it with him afterward I drew his attention to Matt. 12:32 and remarked that I would be afraid to make such an assertion.

Throughout Jesus' earthly life the Holy Spirit had an active role, as is made clear by the words of John the Baptist. "For he whom God has sent utters the words of God, for it is not by measure that he gives the Spirit; the Father loves the Son, and has given all things into his hand" (John 3:34-35). Or, according to Phillips, "the one whom God sent speaks the authentic words of God, and there can be no measuring of the Spirit given to *him*." In other words, Jesus Christ was indwelt by the Holy Spirit in a degree that was limitless and beyond measure. Jesus knew the fullness of the Holy Spirit because both were part of the Trinity, and because He was utterly holy and without sin.

71

THE DEATH OF JESUS CHRIST

When we think of the death of Jesus Christ we know that it came about not by unfortunate circumstances, but by the express design of God. Pontius Pilate, the Roman judge who ordered Jesus to be crucified, spoke with all the self-confidence of ignorance when he asked Jesus, "Do you not know that I have power to release you, and power to crucify you?" (John 19:10). Jesus answered him, "You would have no power over me unless it had been given you from above." The crucifixion came as no unexpected shock to Jesus or to the Father. As Jesus had already said, "For this reason the Father loves me, because I lay down my life, that I may take it again. No one takes it from me, but I lay it down of my own accord. I have power to lay it down, and I have power to take it again" (John 10:17-18).

In Hebrews we read about "the blood of Christ, who *through the eternal Spirit* offered himself without blemish to God . . ." (Heb. 9:14, italics mine). Just as the Holy Spirit had been active in the incarnation and life of Christ, so also He was active in His death and atonement. Both John Owen and George Smeaton devote a good deal of space to the consideration of this somewhat controversial verse, but one sentence of Smeaton's is enough to sum up its implication. "The Son of God, moved and animated by the Holy Ghost, offered Himself without spot as an atoning sacrifice."[1]

This verse in Hebrews 9 occurs in a passage of Scripture where the writer is comparing the first tabernacle in the wilderness with its sacrifices, priests, etc., with the greater and more perfect Tabernacle which is the body of Jesus Christ. The writer says of the old tabernacle, with all its sacrifices and priests, that "according to this arrangement, gifts and sacrifices are offered which cannot perfect the conscience of the worshiper" (Heb. 9:9). The whole chapter is worth studying, but we learn four things from verse 14:

[1]George Smeaton, *The Holy Spirit* (London: Banner of Truth, 1958), p. 132.

1. Christ shed His blood.
2. He was without blemish.
3. This purifies our consciences.
4. It was all made possible by the eternal Holy Spirit.

It is easy to overlook the fact that the atoning death of Christ was made possible by the Holy Spirit, but this is a wonderful and important revelation. It would be sad if we missed it.

It is profitable to remember that in the most sacred recesses of the old tabernacle was the Holy of Holies. No man or priest could ever enter it except the high priest, and he only once a year. Inside the Holy of Holies were a number of objects: 1. The alter of incense; 2. The ark of the covenant in which were the urn or pot of manna, Aaron's rod that budded, and the two tables of stone on which God's law was written; 3. The mercy seat (which was the gold lid of the ark). Two notable items of furniture were missing. First, the tabernacle had no windows and no lamp because the glory of the Lord filled the Holy of Holies. Second, there was no seat in the Holy of Holies because the high priest's work was never finished; he never had an opportunity to sit down. There is only one high priest of whom it is written that He finished His work *and sat down,* and that is Jesus Christ. "When he had made purification for sins, he sat down at the right hand of the Majesty on high" (Heb. 1:3).

John, writing his account of Jesus Christ's death, told us that when Jesus had received the vinegar, He said, " *'It is finished';* and he bowed his head and gave up his spirit" (John 19:30, italics mine).

All this was made possible by the eternal Holy Spirit, and its implications for us are indeed far-reaching. In John 7:38-39 Jesus preached that "he who believes in me, as the scripture has said, 'Out of his heart shall flow rivers of living water.'" The apostle John adds, "Now this he said about the Spirit, which those who believed in him were to receive; for as yet the Spirit had not been given, because Jesus was not yet glorified."

In the twelfth chapter of John we get a glimpse of what was

meant by Jesus being "glorified." "The hour has come for the Son of man to be *glorified.* Truly, truly, I say to you, unless a grain of wheat *falls into the earth and dies,* it remains alone; *but if it dies,* it bears much fruit" (John 12:23-24, italics mine).

These two passages make it clear that it was essential for Jesus to die before the Holy Spirit could be poured out in fullness upon believers. This could come only after the cleansing and atoning work of Jesus was finished.

THE RESURRECTION OF JESUS CHRIST

We have seen how in all the life and work of Jesus Christ the Holy Spirit played a crucial role. This is true also of the resurrection of the Lord.

It is particularly important that we think rightly about the Resurrection because it was the key message of the apostles. If they had merely preached "Christ crucified" they would have caused no ripples. The Jews and Romans alike would gladly have assented to such teaching. And it was historically undeniable in any case. It was as they preached the fact that Jesus had been raised from the dead that they stirred up opposition against themselves.

This message not only gave rise to criticism and persecution; it was the supreme message of triumph of the New Testament. Paul no more than stated a plain truth when he wrote, "If Christ has not been raised, then our preaching is in vain and your faith is in vain" (1 Cor. 15:14).

We have seen that Jesus said that He laid down His life and He took it up again, and in Acts 2:32 Peter stated "that God raised Him up. It is also true that Jesus Christ was raised from death by the Holy Spirit. This should cause us no confusion because of the Scriptural practice of ascribing the same operation: sometimes to the Father, sometimes to the Son and then to the Holy Spirit."[2]

---

[2]T. C. Hammond, *In Understanding Be Men* (Leicester, England: Inter-Varsity Press, and used by permission of InterVarsity Press, U.S.A., 1968), p. 132.

The Holy Spirit in the Gospels

Paul wrote to the Romans that "if the Spirit of him who raised Jesus from the dead dwells in you, he who raised Christ Jesus from the dead will give life to your mortal bodies also through his Spirit which dwells in you" (Rom. 8:11). This is endorsed by Peter: "Christ also died for sins once for all, the righteous for the unrighteous, that he might bring us to God, being put to death in the flesh but made alive in the spirit" (1 Peter 3:18).

FOR DISCUSSION

1. What did John the Baptist lack that humble believers can enjoy?
2. Was the Incarnation an act of God the Father, God the Son, or God the Holy Spirit?
3. Give one or more Bible passages that make it clear that the Holy Spirit was active in the Incarnation.
4. Have we sometimes neglected the humanity of Jesus Christ?
5. In the case of Jesus Christ did a process of growth take place, or was it unnecessary and impossible?
6. What part did the Holy Spirit play in the baptism of Jesus Christ?
7. What was the purpose of the baptism of Jesus Christ?
8. After the temptation of Jesus Christ He read the Scriptures in the synagogue. Did the Holy Spirit have a role in this?
9. In this public reading from Scripture what Old Testament prophecy was fulfilled?
10. Did the Holy Spirit have a role in the earthly ministry of the Lord Jesus Christ?
11. Name three things concerning the death of Christ that are referred to in Hebrews 9:14.
12. Did the Holy Spirit have a role in the resurrection of Jesus Christ?

8

The Holy Spirit and Pentecost

The Book of Acts is sometimes called the Acts of the Holy Spirit, and bearing in mind that in the first thirteen chapters of Acts there are forty references to the Holy Spirit this seems quite appropriate. The book was written by Luke who was a physician by profession, and his scientific training shows itself in the way he observes and records the early and vital experiences of the young church.

The words "Pentecost" and "Pentecostal" are used in so many different ways, from describing a denomination to explaining a personal experience, that it often is difficult to understand exactly what they mean.

Pentecost was originally a Jewish festival and an important one. It was instituted by God in the time of Moses and is described in Leviticus 23:15-21. It took place fifty days after Passover week. Without the Passover there would be no way of determining the date of Pentecost. It was a Jewish harvest thanksgiving and was linked to the Passover, which is particularly appropriate. Without the atoning death of Christ at the Jewish feast of Passover, there could have been no outpouring of the Holy Spirit as recorded in Acts 2. Without the crucifixion, Pentecost would have been impossible; without Pentecost the crucifixion would have been a wasted extravagance.

Let us try to picture the scene in Jerusalem during Pentecost. The city would have been bursting at the seams with people. It was one of the three most important festivals in the Jewish year, and all males who lived within a radius of twenty miles from Jerusalem were obliged by Jewish law to attend.

The festival took place at a time of year when travel was easiest, and people would come from far and wide. The list of home towns and countries as given in Acts 2:8-11 gives us a good idea of what a bustling and cosmopolitan scene it must have been. People from Cyrene in Libya, Egypt, Mesopotamia, Asia, Rome, and many other places were there. The crowd consisted not only of Jews by birth, but also of proselytes, Gentiles who had grown weary of their pagan religion and had converted to Judaism. There would have been almost as many people as at the Passover, and possibly more.

The followers of Jesus in Jerusalem numbered 120 (Acts 1:15), but that did not include all the believers in the country, because we learn from 1 Corinthians 15:6 that after the Resurrection Jesus appeared to more than 500 brethren at one time. G. Campbell Morgan suggests that the rest of the brethren were guilty of disobedience by not being present in Jerusalem, and therefore missed the blessing of Pentecost. This is not necessarily so. The apostles were in Jerusalem at the time of the crucifixion and resurrection and they were also there seven weeks later for Pentecost, but Jesus gave repeated instructions for them to travel to Galilee between these two occasions (Matt. 28:7,10,16; Mark 16:7). Why was it so important for them to pay a visit to Galilee? It is almost certain that the greatest concentration of believers was in Galilee, since that was where Jesus had spent most time ministering, and there were two vital things that they needed. First, they needed to be convinced of the fact of the Resurrection; second, they needed to hear the Great Commission. I believe that it was on the mountain on Galilee that Jesus appeared to more than 500 brethren at once (Matt. 28:16-20).

G. Campbell Morgan also stresses the fact that most commentators assume that the 120 who waited in Jerusalem spent their time in praying for the gift of the Holy Spirit. We are certainly sure that they spent their time in prayer, because this is documented by the careful observer Luke, in Acts 1:14, but he does not state what they prayed for. The prayer for the Holy Spirit was prayed by Jesus Christ. "I will pray the Father, and he will give you another Counselor, to be with you for ever, even the Spirit of truth, whom the world cannot receive, because it neither sees him nor knows him; you know him, for he dwells with you, and will be in you" (John 14:16-17).

The disciples were in prayer and they were "of one accord." There was a great sense of unity and a spirit of prayer. So the scene was set for the day of the birth of the church; a city crowded with perhaps 2 1/2 to 3 million people from wide and varied geographic locations, and 120 believers in Jesus united in prayer. With so many tourists in the city the news of anything that happened was bound to spread rapidly throughout the then known world, "every nation under heaven" (Acts 2:5).

It was 9:00 in the morning and the city was coming to life. Without warning, a noise of a mighty wind, such as we associate with a hurricane or tornado, was heard. Unlike a tornado however, there was no actual wind, but only the sound of it. This sound filled the meeting place of the believers, and it was so mighty that it brought the people in their thousands to where the disciples were gathered.

The sights and sounds were so extraordinary that the people were utterly bewildered. In addition to the noise like that of a gale there appeared tongues like fire sitting on each of the little flock of disciples. And they were all filled with the Holy Spirit.

The person of the Holy Spirit Himself was invisible, but the sound of wind and sight of fire would have made an indelible impression on those who witnessed them. They are both clear symbols of the Holy Spirit. We are reminded again of Genesis 1:2, and the fact that in the account of the Creation we learn that the Spirit of God (or, to quote the New English Bible, "a mighty wind") "was moving over the face of the waters." So in the beginning of the creation story and also in the beginning of the church the Holy Spirit was involved.

To say that the disciples were transformed is to state the obvious, but it is important. These men were no strangers to spiritual power, as we learn from their testimony in Luke

10:17. "Lord, even the demons are subject to us in your name." However, they now experienced a completely new dimension that had been unknown before. Just before His death Jesus, speaking of the Holy Spirit, had said to them, "He dwells *with* you, and will be *in* you" (John 14:17, italics mine).

"And they were all filled with the Holy Spirit" (Acts 2:4). The transformation that had *not* taken place in three years of teaching and example by Jesus Christ, took place in a moment when the Holy Spirit was poured out. After the Resurrection it was not more information they needed but more power, and at Pentecost they received it in abundance in the person of the Holy Spirit. These were the men and women who had been paralyzed by fear after the Resurrection; now they dominated Jerusalem and the whole area surrounding it.

At Pentecost the church was born and individuals were born again. Ever afterward it was possible for men and women who accepted Jesus Christ as Savior to become the "temple of the Holy Spirit." It would take time for all the implications to be fully understood, but what took place that day made the Jerusalem temple obsolete, as the atoning death of Christ made the function of the priests irrelevant.

Before Pentecost the disciples were as useless as when they were first called. After Pentecost they were men who turned the world upside down. By far the most controversial aspect of Pentecost is the fact that they "began to speak in other tongues, as the Spirit gave them utterance." Some have suggested that this was not so much a miracle of speaking; the disciples spoke as usual, and the miracle that took place was in the hearers who were able to hear in their native languages. This need not be taken too seriously, as the Bible is quite clear in its statement that they "began to speak in other tongues."

A more serious suggestion is that the gift was necessary as a means of evangelizing those who came from "all the nations under heaven." It is important to know that virtually all those in Jerusalem, including the apostles, spoke both Greek and Aramaic. The very Scripture from which Jesus quoted was a

Greek translation of the Hebrew Old Testament. Since they spoke a common tongue there was no actual need for interpretation.

We shall deal with the gift of tongues in a later chapter, but we must look a little more closely at this gift as recorded in Acts 2.

The sound of a mighty wind had brought the people together, and they may or may not have seen the tongues that were so much like fire. These were certainly great "attention getters," and when they arrived on the scene the outsiders were bewildered because they heard all the followers of Jesus speaking in other languages. So many strange and unexpected things were happening that it was small wonder they were puzzled. As they listened more carefully they realized that the believers were speaking in languages unfamiliar to the speakers, but known to the hearers from Babylon, Asia Minor, Crete, Arabia, Rome, etc. The believers were speaking in foreign languages but what were they speaking about? It is clear from Acts 2:11 that they were "telling in our own tongues the mighty works of God."

It is too often overlooked that the way in which the gift of tongues was used at Pentecost was not so much for evangelism as for praising God. Although the foreign languages were not a practical necessity for evangelizing the "all nations," they were another indication that God was interested in others besides those who lived in Israel. It would take time before that lesson was absorbed by the apostles.

The behavior change in the once-timid disciples was so great that it is not surprising that some mockers scoffed that they were drunk. It is of passing interest to remember the words of Paul: "Do not get drunk with wine, for that is debauchery; but be filled with the Spirit" (Eph. 5:18). J. Oswald Sanders has written:

These were indeed God intoxicated men. The observers were nearer the truth than they knew, for there are some striking correspondences between the stimulation of wine and the stimulus of the Holy Spirit.[1]

The gift of tongues at Pentecost was not a practical necessity for evangelism but it made an indelible impression, first on the disciples and then on the observers. It was meant to be a sign that God had done something special. We read that Peter "lifted up his voice." He would certainly need to, bearing in mind the size of the audience. It is helpful to take a modern paraphrase such as Phillips and to try to read Peter's sermon as if you never read it before. We do not have a record of all that he said (v. 40), but several things are clear. He was a master of the Old Testament; at once connecting what had taken place with the prophecy of Joel. He was master of his audience. Most significant of all he was master of himself, all because of the miraculous change that had taken place with the fullness of the Holy Spirit.

The theme of this first sermon set the tone of those that were to follow. Peter stressed the fact that Jesus was the Messiah and that He had been raised from the dead. He also stressed that the Holy Spirit had been poured out, and did not hesitate to promise that the Holy Spirit would be given to those who repented and were baptized (vv. 38-39). The fact that 3,000 obeyed and were baptized is certainly proof that what had taken place was of God.

Verse 42 mentions that the 3,000 devoted themselves to the apostles' teaching. This must have involved a great deal of organization. It was the first step of obedience in fulfilling the commission of Jesus Christ, "Go therefore and make disciples of all nations, baptizing them in the name of the Father and of the Son and of the Holy Spirit, *teaching them* to observe all that I have commanded you" (Matt. 28:19-20, italics mine).

The change in the lives of the 3,000 was as striking a proof

[1]J. Oswald Sanders, *The Holy Spirit and His Gifts* (Grand Rapids: Zondervan, 1940), p. 52.

as was the change in the disciples, that God had ushered in a great new period in the "age of the Holy Spirit." God be praised that the promise was not only to them but is to us also. We too can repent, believe, and appropriate the fullness of the Holy Spirit.

FOR DISCUSSION

1. What kind of Jewish festival was Pentecost?
2. Why was it important for the disciples to go to Galilee after the Resurrection?
3. How many days elapsed between the Passover and Pentecost?
4. Did the disciples experience spiritual power before Pentecost?
5. Was the gift of tongues given to the disciples so that they could communicate the gospel to foreigners who did not speak the local language?
6. Why was the gift of tongues given at Pentecost?
7. How many responded to the events of Pentecost and to Peter's preaching?

9

The Holy Spirit
and the Apostolic Church

One of the keys to understanding the developments of the apostolic church is found in Acts 1:8: "You shall receive power when the Holy Spirit has come upon you; and you shall be my witnesses in Jerusalem and in all Judea and Samaria and to the end of the earth." The latter part of this verse is often quoted as a missionary commission, but it is less a commission than a promise. It was not stated that they *"must"* be witnesses but that they *"will,"* and of course that was exactly what happened. The events of Pentecost and directly after were not part of a plan carefully contrived by the disciples; rather they were carried along by the Holy Spirit. The first attempts at evangelism were about as carefully planned as a forest fire!

It is clear from succeeding chapters that the disciples were still far from understanding the promise of Jesus Christ. They were very slow to comprehend that their witnessing was to include Samaria and the end of the earth.

As they left Mount Olivet for the half-mile walk back to Jerusalem they had much food for thought. Not only had they been told again of the promise of power, but also of the fact that "this Jesus, who was taken up from you into heaven, will come in the same way as you saw him go into heaven" (Acts 1:11).

We learn that for ten days they devoted themselves to prayer, and then came the mighty outpouring of the Holy Spirit at Pentecost. They had been told several times that they were to wait for the power and they did just that. Many Christians, myself included, have experienced a longing for more power in their life and ministry, and have waited and waited for their own "personal Pentecost." Much heartbreak and behavioral excess has often been caused by this. Often people are urged to seek and to wait for the Holy Spirit. Under this pressure and out of desperation some extreme practices have taken place, when what was needed was quiet appropriation. We can no more have our own Pentecost than we can have our personal incarnation in the Bethlehem stable. We can and should enjoy the fruits of these events, but they were a once-and-for-all experience brought about by a holy God through His precious Son.

I can well remember an experience I had when I was a young Christian. I was introduced to a man in a city on the English Channel, and he began to tell me of a great spiritual experience that he had been through, indicating that I could have the same blessing. He then went on to declare that in this experience a tongue of fire had settled upon him. He offered to remove his jacket and shirt so that I could see the burn scar. I soon excused myself, because despite my inexperience I knew that in the record of Pentecost there were tongues *as of* fire, and there was certainly no record of a need for first-aid treatment!

Many books have been written about the Acts of the Apostles, and a verse-by-verse account would be out of place here. There are at least three things that we should consider: first, the change in the disciples; second, the message of the apostolic church; and third, the spread of the gospel.

THE CHANGE IN THE DISCIPLES

In chapter 8 we looked at the change that took place in Peter as the result of the outpouring of the Holy Spirit at Pentecost, but we must look more closely at the change that took place in others as well. Their behavior is the more striking because it contrasts so vividly with the conduct of the disciples after the crucifixion. Indeed, it seems likely that the disciples' fear before Pentecost was recorded so that the change would be the more noticeable.

The Holy Spirit and the Apostolic Church

In Acts 2 we see Peter utterly at ease and preaching with such effectiveness and power that those who heard "were cut to the heart, and said to Peter and the rest of the apostles, 'Brethren, what shall we do?'"

In chapter 3 we read the account of the healing of the lame man at 3:00 in the afternoon, with another sermon by Peter. Again many were convinced and converted and "the number of the men came to about five thousand"; and that was without counting their families. As a result of this Peter and John were cast into prison and the next day interrogated by rulers, elders, scribes, and the high priest and his family.

This was a situation which would normally have been most intimidating. Peter and John were completely outnumbered. Many of the council had been responsible for the death of Jesus Christ. The disciples were unsophisticated fishermen of very limited education, and they were surrounded by men of advanced social position and education.

Two verses stand out: "Then Peter, *filled with the Holy Spirit,* said to them . . ." (Acts 4:8, italics mine), and the response of their interrogators: "Now when they saw the boldness of Peter and John, and perceived that they were uneducated, common men, they wondered" (v. 13). They were not bowled over by the personalities of Peter and John; rather the contrary, for they noted that they were "common men." What amazed them was Peter and John's boldness, and we are expressly told that Peter spoke in the power of the Holy Spirit.

It would be possible to continue this line of thought through the whole Book of Acts, but a few more examples must suffice. In chapter 6 we have an account of the selection of seven men who were to be responsible for the practical and menial work of the growing church. We are expressly told that they were "men of good repute, full of the Spirit and of wisdom" (v. 3). We are also told that Stephen was one of them. Some men disputed with Stephen, "but they could not withstand the wisdom and the Spirit with which he spoke" (v. 10).

Thus the triumphant witness continued. The young church was faced with every conceivable obstacle: opposition, persecution, death, demon possession. It faced them all in a manner that can only be described by one word: *authority.* Nothing and no one on earth or in hell could withstand them. In 1 Thessalonians 1:5 Paul writes that "our gospel came to you not only in word, but also in power and in the Holy Spirit and with full conviction."

Consider the shipwreck episode in Acts 27. Paul was being taken as a prisoner to Rome, and the ship sailed from Crete against Paul's advice and despite the fact that it was the stormy season. Soon the ship was in trouble and the sailors selfishly tried to make their escape. Through all these experiences, and more, Paul was in absolute command. He was the one who advised the centurion to keep the sailors from leaving. He was the one who promised them that they would all be safe because God had assured him so. He was the one who realized that exhaustion was one of their enemies and advised them to eat (v. 34). Such was Paul's authority that you would think he was the ship's captain instead of a humble prisoner!

Surely the greatest need of the church today is just that authority. When Christians come from churches in the third world to study in our seminaries, they go away with a good knowledge of psychology, church growth, or fine organization and technique, but it is certain they seldom leave having learned about authority in the Holy Spirit. Indeed many of them have seen more of it in their own countries.

If we go back and examine the great revivals of history we learn that they were characterized by men with enormous spiritual authority that enabled them to stand out like huge rocks in the ebbing tides. Whitefield describes an occasion when he had received an invitation to preach in the church of the spiritual giant, Jonathan Edwards, in Northampton, Massachusetts. Whitefield records that as he preached he could see tears of joy flowing down the face of Edwards as he experienced the authority of the preaching.

Jonathan Edwards was no stranger to the power of the Holy Spirit. Two hundred years ago an enormous revival swept western Massachusetts. Jonathan Edwards had many problems that to us would be insurmountable. He read every word of his sermons, and he was so shortsighted that he had to hold his manuscript close to his face. Yet people often fell to the floor under the convicting power of the Holy Spirit. Secular historians have described him as the greatest philosophic brain ever produced by North America. Such was the spiritual power of his preaching that he was prevailed upon to write a description of its effects. It was published under the title, *A Narrative of Surprising Conversions in New England.* It had a wide circulation and reprints made their way to Great Britain. The effectiveness of his preaching resulted not from the authority of his intellect but from the authority of the Holy Spirit.

What of Whitefield as he preached to 20,000 coal miners in the open air on Hannam Common, Bristol? He was not only able to make himself heard, but preached with such clarity and authority that the tough black-faced miners had streaks of white down their cheeks where the tears of conviction had flowed.

Two hundred years ago a great revival was experienced in America, Great Britain, and elsewhere. In Wales a godly man, Howell Harris, was greatly used. In his diary there are comments like this: "arrived in such and such a place, preached, felt the old authority." He was frank to admit when the authority was lacking, but never content to do without it.

On the rare occasions when authoritative preaching is heard Christians become uncomfortable. When they are looking for a church, they will ask what the nursery facilities are like, how good the Sunday school is, whether there is a good music program. These are just a few of the questions that are asked. Similarly when a church is looking for a pastor, what do *they* want to know? What is his education? Is he a good mixer? Will his wife be an asset? Is he a good visitor? Is he good at administration? When is the question asked, Is he filled with the Holy Spirit and is his preaching authoritative? Seldom. Why? Because we are as uncomfortable with it as the Jews were in the time of Paul.

We are content with our country-club atmosphere, with its entertainment and smooth-running program. No wonder the world does not fear us; it has no need to do so. The preaching of the apostles as well as that of Jesus showed that because they were so humble before God they were mighty before men.

Much of the administration and government of churches today makes this weakness almost impossible to change. The church chooses a man to be its leader and undershepherd. But they pay his salary, and if he says things that offend, his congregation rejects him. The fact of democracy in the church is one of the reasons for this. In no other system does the leader derive his authority from the people under him, rather than from those over him.

This Holy Spirit authority is what is so sorely needed today, and if we turn away from it we are surely grieving the Holy Spirit of God. Of course I do not refer to an abrasiveness that is of the flesh, and which is alien to a man whose authority comes from the Holy Spirit.

Christianity was born for endurance, not an exotic, but a hardy plant, braced by the keen wind; not languid, nor childish, nor cowardly. It walks with a strong step and erect frame. It is kindly, but firm. It is gentle, but honest. It is calm, but not facile; decided, but not churlish. It does not fear to speak the stern word of condemnation against error, not to raise its voice against surrounding evils under the pretext that it is not of this world. It does not shrink from giving honest reproof, lest it come under the charge of displaying an unchristian spirit. It calls sin sin, on whomsoever it is found, and would rather risk the accusation of being actuated by a bad spirit than not discharge an explicit duty.

Let us not misjudge strong words used in honest controversy. Out of the heat a viper may come forth, but we shake it off and feel no harm. The religion of both Old and New Testament is marked by fervent outspoken testimonies against evil. To speak smooth things in such a case may be sentimentalism, but it is not Christianity. If anyone should be frank, manly, honest, cheerful (I do not say blunt or rude, for a Christian must be courteous and polite), it is he who has tasted that the Lord is gracious, and is looking for and hastening unto the coming of the day of God.[1]

This lack of authority is not by any means the fault of preachers alone, but is a condemnation of most of the church of Christ. It should drive us all to a spiritual renewal that will bring with it the New Testament authority.

THE MESSAGE OF THE APOSTLES

We have seen that the whole thrust of Peter's teaching on the day of Pentecost was that Jesus had fulfilled Old Testament prophecy by dying and being raised from the dead, and that this was the reason why the Holy Spirit had been poured out. In the next chapter Peter again preached and once more there was great blessing, but there is a revealing phrase in chapter 4 concerning Peter's message. "The priests and the captain of the temple and the Sadducees came upon them, annoyed because they were teaching the people and proclaiming in Jesus the resurrection from the dead" (4:1-2). After Peter and John had spent the night in prison they were brought before the council, and once again Peter's defense was simply to preach Jesus with immense authority. The council "charged them not to speak or teach at all in the name of Jesus" (v. 18).

In Acts 8 we read that after the martyrdom of Stephen "they were all scattered throughout the region of Judea and Samaria. . . . Now those who were scattered went about preaching the word. Philip went down to a city of Samaria, and proclaimed to them the Christ" (vv. 1, 4-5). Later in that chapter Philip met the eunuch in his chariot: "Then Philip opened his mouth, and beginning with this scripture he told him the good news of Jesus." In Acts 10 we read about Peter's visit to Cornelius. We shall look at this incident again in another chapter. Our purpose here is to observe the message that Peter preached. From beginning to end Peter's message to Cor-

---

[1]Horatius Bonar, *God's Way of Holiness* (Chicago: Moody Press, 1970).

nelius that day was about Jesus. It is a sermon that is worth studying. It took the essential facts of the redemptive death and power of Jesus and presented them to people who were spiritually hungry.

This same theme runs through all the sermons in the Book of Acts. It was also Paul's theme at Mars Hill and elsewhere. When Paul was on trial before Felix he summed up the whole matter by saying, "With respect to the resurrection of the dead I am on trial before you today" (Acts 24:21).

The most dramatic experience the apostles had ever had was that of Pentecost, and it would have been natural if they had been brimming over with what they had experienced of the Holy Spirit. Indeed, judging by what we often see today, they would have spent the rest of their lives repeating the story of this experience, even long after it had been recorded in a book. They did indeed mention the Holy Spirit from time to time, but their message was preeminently that of Jesus and the Resurrection. Often John Wesley, after an exhausting journey on horseback, would preach at a meeting, and after the meeting would write in his diary, "I offered them Jesus." And often his brother Charles recorded similar sentiments in hymns. The following is just one of many.

> Jesus! the name high over all,
>   In hell, or earth, or sky;
> Angels and men before it fall,
>   And devils fear and fly.
>
> O that the world might taste and see
>   The riches of His grace;
> The arms of love that compass me
>   Would all mankind embrace.
>
> His only righteousness I show,
>   His saving grace proclaim;
> 'Tis all my business here below
>   To cry: "Behold the Lamb!"

The Holy Spirit and the Apostolic Church

> Happy, if with my latest breath
> I might but gasp His name;
> Preach Him to all, and cry in death:
> "Behold, behold the Lamb!"

This emphasis upon the person of Jesus Christ was entirely in harmony with Jesus' promise. "When the Spirit of truth comes, he will guide you into all the truth; for he will not speak on his own authority, but whatever he hears he will speak, and he will declare to you the things that are to come. *He will glorify me*" (John 16:13-14, italics mine). The supreme task of the Holy Spirit is not to draw attention to Himself but to glorify Jesus. Let us take to heart the message of the apostolic church, and may it become our theme.

THE SPREAD OF THE APOSTOLIC CHURCH

We saw in Acts 1:8 that Jesus Christ promised the disciples that after receiving the Holy Spirit they would be His witnesses in Jerusalem and in Judea and Samaria and to the end of the earth. We saw that after only two sermons there were 5,000 male believers alone, plus their families. This process of expansion continued in Jerusalem: "None of the rest dared join them, but the people held them in high honor. And more than ever believers were added to the Lord, multitudes both of men and women" (Acts 5:13-14). Then again in the next chapter, "the word of God increased; and the number of the disciples multiplied greatly in Jerusalem, and a great many of the priests were obedient to the faith" (Acts 6:7). Certainly the promise to evangelize Jerusalem was accomplished with immense rapidity.

It was not the city only that knew the impact of the gospel. What was taking place was so amazing that "the people also gathered from the towns around Jerusalem, bringing the sick and those afflicted with unclean spirits, and they were all healed" (Acts 5:16). So we see that the first evangelizing outside Jerusalem did not consist of missionary journeys but of the congregation coming to the believers.

The next great step was the persecution that arose after the stoning of Stephen. The persecution scattered the church but the apostles stayed in the city. This persecution was similar to a man trying to put out a campfire by applying a boot to it. The fire certainly was scattered but each glowing ember simply started another fire. The opposition of men was overruled by God to fulfill His purpose.

One result of this persecution was that Philip went down to Samaria "and proclaimed to them the Christ" (Acts 8:5). As a result multitudes of Samaritans believed. This of course was the more remarkable because of the bitter animosity between them and the Jews.

Another significant development came of this scattering after the death of Stephen. "Now those who were scattered because of the persecution that arose over Stephen traveled as far as Phoenicia and Cyprus and Antioch, speaking the word to none except Jews" (Acts 11:19). This represented a significant spread of the gospel, but evangelism was still seen as being only for the Jewish nation. "But there were some of them, men of Cyprus and Cyrene, who on coming to Antioch spoke to the Greeks also, preaching the Lord Jesus. And the hand of the Lord was with them, and a great number that believed turned to the Lord" (Acts 11:20-21). How appropriate that the Greeks should first hear the gospel from a man from Cyrenaica (in Libya) when it was a man from that place who helped Jesus to carry His cross. It would seem that by this time there had been a great enough accumulation of evidence both from the teaching of Jesus and the experience of the disciples to have convinced all the disciples of the fact that the purposes of God embraced the whole world. They still did not comprehend that God's plan included Gentiles as well as Jews. This, despite the fact that God had expressly told Ananias that Paul "is a chosen instrument of mine to carry my name before the Gentiles and kings and the sons of Israel" (Acts 9:15).

To widen their vision God used a series of incidents which

we read of in Acts 10 and 11. A Roman centurion, an upright and God-fearing man, was told by God that he should send some of his servants to Joppa to ask Peter to return to the home of the centurion. Simultaneously Peter had a vision of animals and reptiles that Jewish law forbade Jews to eat. Then a voice ordered Peter to kill and eat. Peter's reaction was perfectly orthodox when he replied, " 'No, Lord; for I have never eaten anything that is common or unclean.' And the voice came to him again a second time, 'What God has cleansed, you must not call common' " (Acts 10:14-15).

Peter was still thinking about the vision when the Holy Spirit told him that there were men waiting for him downstairs and he was to go with them. This he did, and we notice that he took "some of the brethren with him." This is important because what was to take place was so crucial a development that it needed to be authenticated by witnesses.

When Peter arrived at the home of Cornelius he was greeted warmly, and he observed that many people were gathered. Peter still had doubts but these were soon dispelled. His message was Christ-centered, and then to the amazement of both Peter and his friends "the Holy Spirit fell on all who heard the word. And the believers from among the circumcised who came with Peter were amazed, because the gift of the Holy Spirit had been poured out even on the Gentiles. For they heard them speaking in tongues and extolling God" (Acts 10:44-45).

Soon Peter had to give an explanation to the Christians in Jerusalem. One man could be mistaken, but Peter had with him six brethren who were witnesses. The vision on the rooftop, the instructions to go with them, the gift of the Holy Spirit, and the gift of tongues were so like their own experience at Pentecost that there could be no doubt that it was the will of God that the gospel should include Gentiles as well as Jews. This is why this chapter is so important; God used a series of events not only to bring blessing to Cornelius, but also to convince Peter and the rest that God's purpose was greater than they dreamed. "When they heard this they were silenced.

And they glorified God, saying, 'Then to the Gentiles also God has granted repentance unto life'" (Acts 11:18).

So the Holy Spirit used not only the 120 Jewish believers in Jerusalem, but men of all races and social levels to spread the gospel. In fact, by the year A.D. 100, the gospel had been spread throughout the great Roman Empire. The apostolic church had the authority of the Holy Spirit, their message everywhere was Jesus and the Resurrection, and it spread faster than could have ever been thought possible.

There are lessons for us in this experience. Do we have divine authority in our preaching? If not, let us pray earnestly that we shall have it. Their message was centered on Jesus Christ; is ours? They went everywhere proclaiming the Lord; do we?

For Discussion

1. Were the disciples quick to see the importance of Pentecost regarding the evangelization of other nations?

2. What is one word that describes the behavior of the disciples after Pentecost?

3. Why are present-day churches so little concerned with spiritual authority?

4. What was the distinctive message of the disciples after the Resurrection?

5. What is the supreme task of the Holy Spirit?

6. Does the Acts of the Apostles describe the techniques used by the apostles to spread the gospel?

7. The early Christians went everywhere preaching the gospel. What was one serious omission?

8. When Peter reported to the church leaders in Jerusalem about the regeneration of Cornelius, they accepted his account. Why?

10

The Baptism of the Holy Spirit

The two phrases "the baptism of the Holy Spirit" and "the fullness of the Holy Spirit" represent two of the greatest blessings that can be experienced by man, and yet in the past few years they have not only caused misunderstanding, but have led to disagreement among Christians that has at times been bitter and has caused many divisions.

On occasions when I have been in the company of Christians of a certain view I have used the phrase "the baptism of the Holy Spirit" believing that it was a courtesy to them, and helpful in mutual understanding. At other times in describing the same experience, I have used the term "the fullness of the Holy Spirit." Again my purpose was to assist in communication.

The two phrases have been used by some as being interchangeable, but after much thought and prayer over a period of many years I have come to the conclusion that I should endeavor to state what I believe to be the scriptural meaning of each, and then to use them in that sense. It would be helpful if it was common practice to use the correct biblical phrases in communication, but all too often we have caused confusion by the use of jargon and inexact phraseology.

The term "baptism of the Holy Spirit" often has been used to describe the meaning of a blessing that is received by a person after he has been a Christian for some time, and indeed some would maintain that if a person had not "received the baptism" he would be regarded as a substandard Christian. This is no new problem. G. Campbell Morgan writing well

95

before World War II states: "The term the *baptism of the Spirit* has been very generally misunderstood, and therefore misapplied. It has been used as though it were synonymous with *the filling of the Spirit;* and, consequently, some persons speak of baptism of the Spirit as *a second blessing.* They teach that it is necessary to ask for, and to wait for, and to expect this baptism of the Spirit, as something different from and beyond conversion."[1]

It is vitally important to understand what the Bible means when it speaks of being "baptized by the Spirit." John the Baptist repeatedly preached that, "I baptize you with water for repentance, but he who is coming after me is mightier than I, whose sandals I am not worthy to carry; *he will baptize you with the Holy Spirit and with fire*" (Matt. 3:11, italics mine). In all four gospels John is recorded as repeating similar truth.

It was clearly prophesied that Jesus would baptize with the Spirit, but that is still ambiguous. Paul seems to have put the matter beyond reasonable doubt when he wrote, "For by one Spirit we were all baptized into one body—Jews or Greeks, slaves or free—and all were made to drink of one Spirit" (1 Cor. 12:13). This is merely an extension of the truth uttered by Jesus to Nicodemus, "Truly, truly, I say to you, unless one is born of water and the Spirit, he cannot enter the kingdom of God. That which is born of the flesh is flesh, and that which is born of the Spirit is spirit. Do not marvel that I said to you, 'You must be born anew.' The wind blows where it wills, and you hear the sound of it, but you do not know whence it comes or whither it goes; so it is with every one who is born of the Spirit" (John 3:5-8).

To be baptized by the Spirit is to become a Christian, and if we do not have the Spirit we are not Christians. As Paul exclaims to the Romans, "But you are not in the flesh, you are in the Spirit, if in fact the Spirit of God dwells in you. Any one who does not have the Spirit of Christ does not belong to him" (Rom. 8:9).

---

[1]Morgan, *The Spirit of God,* p. 161.

The Baptism of the Holy Spirit

It is imperative that these phrases be lifted out of controversy and disagreement and that our lives be lived in the penetrating blaze that they give. How often I have rejoiced when Christians have spoken of a new dimension in this life, and as they have revealed what a blessing it is to speak in tongues, but how sad if they must misuse this term "the baptism." I believe that God is doing great new things in our day, but I can see that as long as the insistence remains to use the term "the baptism" it will be exploited by Satan to cause great disagreement among brothers in Christ.

Does the Holy Spirit really live in us? Have we been "baptized by the Spirit into one body and that the body of Christ"? It may well be that we are unsure of these things, that we do not know if the Holy Spirit lives in us. If so, our questions should be like those who heard Peter in the second chapter of Acts on the day of Pentecost. Their question was, " 'Brethren, what shall we do?' And Peter said to them, 'Repent, and be baptized every one of you in the name of Jesus Christ for the forgiveness of your sins; and you shall receive the gift of the Holy Spirit. For the promise is to you and to your children" (vv. 37-39). Before you read another page, you can repent and receive Jesus Christ into your life, and you will receive the gift of the Holy Spirit. What a glorious thing it will be if instead of fighting about the Holy Spirit some accept Him into their lives.

FOR DISCUSSION

1. Are the two phrases the "baptism of the Holy Spirit" and "the fullness of the Holy Spirit" interchangeable?

2. What Bible reference indicates that all Christians are baptized by the Spirit into the church?

3. Can we be Christians without being baptized by the Spirit?

4. If we have not received the "baptism of the Spirit," what should we do?

11

The Fullness of the Holy Spirit

To be baptized by the Spirit is to become a Christian, or to use another phrase, to be "born again." Of course this is the whole reason why Jesus came to earth. He said, "I came that they may have life, and have it abundantly" (John 10:10).

John Stott has pointed out that at Pentecost there were two separate groups of people who received the baptism or gift of the Spirit that day. The first group of 120 had been waiting and praying. The second group of 3,000 had not been waiting, but responded to the witness of the believers and the sermon of Peter.[1]

One fact that is essential to grasp is that it is possible to have been baptized by the Spirit and yet not be "filled with the Spirit." In Acts 5 the story of Ananias and Sapphira indicate that even in the early days of the church there were Christians whose devotion left much to be desired.

In Acts 6 we gain more insight into this when we see that it became necessary to choose seven men to perform relatively menial work in the church. The church was instructed to "pick out from among you seven men of good repute, full of the Spirit and of wisdom" (Acts 6:3). By stressing that the men to be chosen were to be filled with the Spirit and of wisdom, it becomes clear that even among the members of the early church, which by now was numbered in thousands, there were

[1]John R. W. Stott, *The Baptism and Fullness of the Holy Spirit* (London: Inter-Varsity Fellowship, and used by permission of InterVarsity Press, USA, 1975).

some who were filled with the Spirit and others who were not, even though they had been baptized in the Spirit.

It should not surprise us that there were great differences in the qualities of Christian life and experience for we see evidence of it often today. It is noticeable that nowhere in the Bible are Christians urged to be "baptized by the Spirit," but Paul does command the Ephesian Christians to "be filled with the Spirit" (Eph. 5:18).

We have seen that Jesus stated that He came to give life and that the life should be abundant, but there are degrees of spiritual life as there are degrees of physical life. In any hospital there will be people in almost every state of life. There will be the hospital staff who are full of life, and some patients who have hardly any life at all, and many degrees of life between the two extremes. There are many Christians whose spiritual life is so faint that it is hard to know whether they are spiritually alive or dead. One of the mistakes we often make is to confuse spiritual longevity with spiritual growth. A person may have been a Christian for many years but still be weak spiritually. Others may have been born again recently but be bursting with spiritual life, just as a human baby can either be healthy or weak.

Another matter of confusion pertains to spiritual knowledge and spiritual life. A person may have learned spiritual truth as a child in a Christian home and have gone on to learn much more in church and even college or seminary. That person may have much knowledge but very little spiritual life. Possibly one of the greatest problems in church life has always been that there are so many who pass as mature Christians, and yet have little or no real spiritual vitality. Often non-Christians have been put off because of exposure to this type of Christian.

If our spiritual knowledge is weak and poor it may not be our fault because we may be very young as Christians with little opportunity for spiritual learning. If our spiritual *life* is poor it is our own fault *entirely* because Paul orders the Ephesians and us to be filled with the Spirit, and God never commands us to perform something that is beyond our power to achieve.

If we doubt that we are filled with the Spirit then it is for us to confess any known sin and appropriate the fact that we are filled with the Spirit. In the case of many of us we may lack the assurance of the *fullness of the Spirit* for several reasons. In some it is because of confusion from what we have heard from others. I have often heard Christians express doubt that they have the fullness of the Spirit because they have heard that the evidence of the fullness is to speak in tongues.

The gift of tongues has its place with other gifts as we shall see later, but it is definitely no more a proof of spiritual fullness than any other gift. Many sincere Christians in the charismatic movement have caused endless heartache in other Christians and divisions among churches by this error. With the best of intentions it can cause a feeling that Christians who have not spoken in tongues are second-rate Christians. Divisions through this emphasis have not only marred Christian witness in home churches but have also caused endless division on the mission field.

Charismatic Christians are much more ready to claim for themselves that they are filled with the Spirit, whereas many non-charismatic Christians who are walking in fellowship with the Lord seem to feel that it is immodest or boastful to actually say that they are filled with the Spirit. This is just as mistaken as to think that it is boastful to say that they are Christians. Neither has anything to be proud of. It simply means that God has spoken to us by His grace and we have responded.

I recall early in my first pastorate that a devoted Christian career girl came to me feeling that although she was aware of no unconfessed sin in her life she was afraid that she was not filled with the Spirit because she had never led anyone else to Christ. At the time I was confused myself about the matter and could do little to help her except to pray for her, and promise that I would study my Bible carefully to try to find the solution.

I had been a Christian for only a few weeks when the Lord began to use me to bring others to Himself and I had made the serious mistake of assuming that every other Christian should have the same experience. I was soon able to inform this girl that leading people to Christ was a spiritual gift and that not all

Christians were called to be soul winners, although all Christians are called to witness. For years I had confused witnessing with evangelism, but I know now that witnessing is not necessarily the same as being a soul winner.

All Christians are not called to be soul winners although in many circles there is a mistaken impression that they must be. Often Christians have suffered agonies of self-reproach until this fact has been explained, and then they have had a wonderful sense of release when these truths have been understood. It is important to emphasize once again that we are all called to *witness* by life and by word.

Some of these problem matters seem to come in cycles and I well remember how embarrassed I was when as a young Christian I was asked publicly, "Is it possible to live a victorious life?" I knew I was expected to say yes, and I knew the exact terms I should have used, but I could not utter them. Perhaps I was too literal, but to me a victorious life meant 100 percent victory 100 percent of the time—which is perfection. I knew I fell far short of that. I still feel that this phrase "victorious life" is often misunderstood and I prefer to use the phrase "a life of fellowship." The fellowship with God may be marred by disobedience or sin but can be restored instantly by confession to the Lord and accepting His forgiveness.

I believe there is a parallel with the fullness of the Spirit. It should be the normal life for a Christian but if it is marred by failure, as at times it will be, it can be immediately restored and renewed by dealing with it before the Lord, and the normal fullness of fellowship will be enjoyed.

Many people accept the Lord as Savior and are baptized into the Spirit, and it may be much later when as the result of teaching, etc., they become filled with the Spirit. This has been the experience of many of us. In the case of many others, particularly in the charismatic movement, they may have been religious, and even ordained, when they were first exposed to the full truth of the Holy Spirit and received the baptism of the Spirit thus becoming Christians, and also received the fullness of the Spirit simultaneously.

One of the greatest dangers is that of considering our own

experience as a model for everyone else. This is one of the pitfalls of emphasizing Christian testimonies too much. We are not called to have someone else's experience. God treats us all as individuals and we should expect only experiences promised in the Bible. All too often things that we have long regarded as valid for Christians have no real basis in the Bible.

We cannot have another baptism in the Spirit because that is a once-for-all experience when we become Christians, but we can have fresh fillings of the Spirit. In an old but useful phrase, "There is one baptism but many fillings."

When I have heard friends who came from a non-Christian background or from a Roman Catholic or Episcopalian church describe their experience in "receiving the baptism," in most cases what they are in fact describing is an experience of regeneration that was also accompanied by a filling of the Spirit.

FOR DISCUSSION

1. Is it possible to have been "baptized by the Spirit" without being "filled by the Holy Spirit"?

2. Were there some members of the early church who were not filled with the Holy Spirit? Give illustrations.

3. Does the Bible urge us to be "baptized by the Holy Spirit"?

4. Does the Bible urge us to be "filled with the Holy Spirit"? Give a Bible reference.

5. Do Christians vary in their spiritual lives?

6. What connection is there between spiritual life and spiritual knowledge?

7. Whose fault is it if our spiritual life is weak and poor?

8. Is the gift of tongues a proof that we are "filled with the Holy Spirit"?

9. Are all Christians called to be soul winners?

10. Would you describe yourself as being filled with the Holy Spirit? If not, why not?

12

Spiritual Warfare

Many people have the impression that once they have been baptized by the Spirit and have become real Christians, the major difficulties of their life are over, and their future life will be one of continuous joy and blessing. These ideas often have been received from the evangelist or person who led them to know the Lord, or can even be a natural feeling that once they have made peace with God through Jesus Christ then all their problems would be resolved. Such people are headed for a rude awakening. It is certainly true that when the Holy Spirit comes to live in us He gives joy and peace that the world can neither give nor take away. It is also true that while we are on earth we battle evil as well as enjoy good.

Paul writes, "For the desires of the flesh are against the Spirit, and the desires of the Spirit are against the flesh; for these are opposed to each other, to prevent you from doing what you would" (Gal. 5:17). Although our personality has become the home of the Holy Spirit it has also become a battleground between the Holy Spirit and the power of self and Satan that has ruled us for so long.

The Bible has a good deal to say about the flesh. Jesus said, "Truly, truly, I say to you, unless one is born of water and the Spirit, he cannot enter the kingdom of God. That which is born of the *flesh is flesh,* and that which is born of the Spirit is spirit" (John 3:5-6). Paul wrote to the Romans, "I know that nothing good dwells within me, that is, in my flesh" (Rom. 7:18), and again, "those who are in the flesh *cannot please God*" (Rom. 8:8, italics mine).

When the Holy Spirit comes to live in our personality it means that our lives take on a whole new dimension. If the King of Kings is living within us the most mundane chore is invested with a new significance. How then can these two conflicting ideas become reconciled? Paul wrote to the Galatians that before becoming a Christian a person is ruled by self alone. When the Holy Spirit takes up residence there are two influences, the flesh and the Spirit, death and life, darkness and light, Satan and God. In some Christians the flesh is uppermost, and in others the Spirit is predominant.

We are urged by Paul to be "filled with the Spirit," but the Spirit can fill only as much of our lives as we make available to Him. If we take a drinking glass and fill it with gravel and then hold it under a water faucet, the water will filter down between the particles of gravel and the glass will soon be filled to overflowing. We can make room for more water only by getting rid of more and more gravel. No analogy is complete, but this may help us to understand one aspect of spiritual truth. The Spirit fills as much of us as we make available to Him. He cannot fill what is already filled with sin and self. This is one of the reasons why Paul has given us lists of characteristics of the flesh so we can recognize them and get rid of them. One of these lists is in Galatians: "Now the works of the flesh are plain: immorality, impurity, licentiousness, idolatry, sorcery, enmity, strife, jealousy, anger, selfishness, dissension, party spirit, envy, drunkenness, carousing, and the like" (Gal. 5:19-21). The New English Bible translates this list as follows: "Anyone can see the kind of behavior that belongs to the lower nature: fornication, impurity, and indecency; idolatry and sorcery; quarrels, a contentious temper, envy, fits of rage, selfish ambitions, dissensions, party intrigues, and jealousies; drinking bouts, orgies, and the like." As we read this catalog it is a shock to know that selfish ambition is included along with fornication, quarrels with drinking bouts, contentious temper with orgies.

There is a need for self-examination so that we may recognize what parts of our life are of the flesh and therefore can be dealt with by confession. This is not meant to advocate morbid introspection. We need to examine our lives for just as long as it takes to deal with sin, and then to enjoy fullness of the Spirit and of fellowship. There is no need to wait until we *feel* sorry. Repentance is not a matter of emotion but of the will. There is often a subtle device of Satan that we can earn forgiveness by remorse. Such ideas are erroneous and damaging.

The normal Christian life is one that is filled with the Spirit and this can be experienced at the time we experienced baptism in the Spirit or it can take place later. Moreover, there can be special fillings for special needs as we see in the early church. "And when they had prayed, the place in which they were gathered together was shaken; and they were all filled with the Holy Spirit and spoke the word of God with boldness" (Acts 4:31).

To be filled with the Spirit is an experience that the youngest Christian should enjoy but it is not a static thing. We shall never reach the place where there is no more to learn or to experience. As we progress, God will reveal more and more what needs to be yielded to Him and to be filled.

It is right that we should rejoice that the Holy Spirit is in us, and wants to fill us, but we must remember that He is a person and can be grieved like any other person. We grieve Him by obstinate disobedience and also by sheer neglect. If we know that we have grieved Him let us apologize and enjoy His fullness once again.

The Bible also tells us, "Do not quench the Spirit" (1 Thess. 5:19). Quench is a word that is used in connection with a fire. To quench a fire is to put it out, and it is significant that Paul wrote to a group of Christians at Thessalonica where the fire of the Holy Spirit was burning with wonderful intensity. However, he had to warn them to be careful not to put the fire out, but to keep it burning.

To return to the conflict between the flesh and the Spirit referred to in Galatians let us remember that there is a promise, "But I say, walk by the Spirit, and do not gratify the desires of the flesh" (Gal. 5:16). There is at least a hint here that if we walk by the Spirit we shall not fulfill the works of the flesh. It is a glorious fact revealed in the New Testament that a life of spiritual fullness is God's will for us. Let us not settle for a second best.

FOR DISCUSSION

1. Is it true that once we have received the "baptism of the Holy Spirit" our major problems are over?

2. When does our personality become the home of the Holy Spirit?

3. How much of us can the Holy Spirit fill?

4. Is repentance a matter of the will or of the emotions?

5. Is the fullness of the Holy Spirit a full and final experience or will there still be room for progress?

6. Is the fullness of the Holy Spirit an experience that should be enjoyed by every Christian? Are you filled with the Spirit?

13

The Gifts of the Holy Spirit in General

Few things are more exciting and rewarding for a Christian than to do the impossible through the power of the Holy Spirit. That has been the experience innumerable times of some Christians, both in the New Testament and in contemporary times. I was once present at a press conference held by Billy Graham, at the University of Illinois at Urbana. He expertly fielded some tough questions from reporters, and then one asked, "Dr. Graham, why do you think that you have been so successful in your work?" The reply was immediate: "When I get to heaven that is the first question that I am going to ask God." Repeatedly Billy Graham has made it clear that the secret of his effectiveness is that God is working through him.

When Jesus appeared to the apostles on Mount Olivet, as recorded in Acts 1, He gave them a task to carry out that was totally beyond their ability: "You shall be my witnesses in Jerusalem and in all Judea and Samaria and to the end of the earth" (Acts 1:8). The track record of the apostles up to this point was dismal and the task before them was impossible in terms of their own human abilities and resources, but Jesus made it clear that this ability to witness would be possible only because "You shall receive power when the Holy Spirit has come upon you. . . ."

For too many years the church has acted as if the Holy Spirit and Christian service are hardly related. It has been assumed that if a man is carefully educated and trained he is automatically qualified to be a pastor, in much the same way a person goes through an educational process and eventually emerges as an engineer or a doctor. Charles Spurgeon had no such illusion. He began his first pastorate when he was sixteen years of age and his ministry was so blessed by God that at eighteen he was called to pastor a large church in London. Eventually he established a theological seminary which he named the Pastor's College (now named Spurgeon's College). He allowed no man to be accepted for the college unless he had already been preaching for two years. Spurgeon commented, "I cannot make a preacher; only God can do that." He stressed that he would be pleased to give training to those already so gifted by God.

I read this as a teenager, while I was busy in my spare time preaching in the part of South London where Spurgeon had been so greatly used of God. Many years later I was fascinated to discover, while preaching in Central America, that the Assemblies of God had taken a similar approach. They had developed it into a carefully planned training program for their national pastors. Always they were looking for evidence that the person being trained was being used by the Lord in ministry. Each advanced section of the course of study depended on the man's continuing effectiveness in applying and using the gifts and training he had previously received.

We shall look at individual gifts in chapter 15, but it seems important to deal with them here in a general way. This will be easier then to compare and contrast them with spiritual fruits. Much confusion has arisen because spiritual gifts have not been considered in relation to fruits; it is almost impossible to have a correct idea of either gifts or fruits unless they are carefully considered together, as they are in 1 Corinthians 12, 13, and 14. Again we must beware that we do not stress the gifts at the expense of the giver. There are many gifts but one Spirit.

ARE SPIRITUAL GIFTS FOR TODAY?

There is a wide divergence of opinion as to whether or not spiritual gifts are actually valid for today. There are several problems in dealing with this subject but I need mention only two.

The first problem is that there are so many different views. Sometimes one view differs only slightly from another.

The second problem is that the views of many who have spoken and written on the subject have understandably changed over a period of years. For example, the views advanced by John R. W. Stott in 1975 are different from his of 1964.[1]

There are those who state that "the gifts were for the apostolic church and any manifestation of them today is of the devil." Others feel that the gift of teaching is the only gift that remains in operation today. The usual view of the Pentecostals is that there are only nine gifts, and then there are extreme views of those who teach that almost anything can be a spiritual gift, including the ability to write poetry or produce television programs.

There is no clear-cut teaching in Scripture that the gifts would pass away. If such a significant change were the will of God, it is reasonable to suppose that there would be clear teaching in the Bible to prepare Christians for that change. Against this scriptural silence concerning the withdrawal of the gifts there stand several positive statements concerning the gifts: "Earnestly desire the higher gifts" (1 Cor. 12:31). "To each is given the manifestation of the Spirit" (1 Cor. 12:7). "Make love your aim, and earnestly desire the spiritual gifts, especially that you may prophesy" (1 Cor. 14:1). "Do not forbid speaking in tongues" (1 Cor. 14:39).

In the light of this it is surprising to read John Walvoord: *"While most of the Church will agree that certain spiritual gifts*

---

[1]Since writing the above my attention has been drawn to the foreword of the 1975 edition where he states that his views are unchanged from the 1964 edition. After rereading the 1975 edition and comparing it with the 1964; and with personal conversations with him between 1964 and 1967, I find it difficult to accept the statement that his views have not changed. I believe that they have.

were discontinued after the apostolic age, others are insisting that gifts given at the beginning of the Church age continue in the same way throughout the entire period"[2] (italics mine).

I can find no evidence in the Bible that spiritual gifts have passed away. I can only repeat, and endeavor to obey, Paul's advice to "earnestly desire the higher gifts" (1 Cor. 12:31). Most, if not all, spiritual gifts can be abused by man or used by Satan, from the gift of tongues to the gift of teaching. Most people who complain about the extravagances of those who speak in tongues or practice the ministry of healing, seem blissfully unaware that perhaps the most misused gift of all is that of teaching. Teaching has so often been degraded and used to persuasively advocate humanism and liberal theology.

In seeking gifts it is essential to be certain that our motives are right. Almost immediately after I became a Christian at about sixteen years of age, God began to use me to lead others to faith in Jesus Christ through personal conversations. At almost the same time I began to accept speaking engagements (preaching is far too grand a word to describe it). I soon ceased to accept these opportunities to speak and my older brother asked why. "I am not seeing people come to Christ through my speaking," I retorted, "so I shall stick to personal evangelism. I am not prepared to be a second-rate preacher for anyone." "What is your motive for speaking?" asked my brother. "To save souls," I replied. "I think you had better spend some more time in prayer until you have got your priorities right," he advised. I did so with reluctance. Eventually God brought me to the position where I told Him that I would speak if it was His will, even if it meant being a second-rate, or even a fifth-rate speaker. I have often been tempted to feel that God took my prayer almost too literally! Invitations to preach began to flow in and I have often marveled at His grace in using such a reluctant and unworthy person to be His messenger.

If we want to be of more use in the service of the Lord it is

[2]John F. Walvoord, *The Holy Spirit at Work Today* (Chicago: Moody, 1973), p. 41.

important that we get our priorities right. For many of us the most natural thing to do is to read a "How to" book, try to put it into practice, and then ask God to bless our efforts. We need to reverse this process. First of all, "earnestly desire the higher gifts." The giver of the gifts is the Holy Spirit; we need first to go to Him and ask Him to give us one or several of the more important spiritual gifts. Whether or not the gift is given is for God to decide. We may ask but not demand, for we do not know enough to know what is best for God's work or for our own good. If the gift is given in answer to prayer, by all means let us strive to use it as fully and as skilfully as possible, but let us never forget it is a gift and therefore nothing to boast about. There are several lists of spiritual gifts in the New Testament. The most important are found in 1 Corinthians 12, Romans 12, and Ephesians 4. There is a reference to the importance of using gifts carefully in 1 Peter 4:10-11. The New Testament lists at least twenty gifts, but it seems that 1 Corinthians 12 is the only place where the gifts are listed in order of priority. Although this list is not exhaustive it is important, because Paul is writing to a very superficial church that seems to have been overly preoccupied with the more sensational gifts. He apparently sets out to give balanced teaching and to help the believers view the whole subject from a true perspective.

First, Paul stresses that although there are many gifts there is only one Spirit. He expounds this in 1 Corinthians 12:4-13. It is important to remember that we should be more concerned with the Spirit Himself than with the gifts.

Second, in verses 14-26 of the same chapter Paul stresses the importance of each member and his gifts, and reminds his readers that none can say any gifts are unimportant.

Third, Paul lists nine gifts in order of importance. It is significant that the first three places are given to apostles, prophets, and teachers. The last place is assigned to the gift of tongues. This is then followed by the exhortation to "earnestly desire the higher gifts." The thrust of chapters 12 and 14 is that no gift should be disparaged, but that some gifts are of more benefit than others to the well-being and growth of the church.

It is these that should be coveted. According to Paul the gift of tongues has a place but a relatively unimportant one, and it certainly should not be allowed to overshadow other gifts.

SPIRITUAL GIFTS AND NATURAL TALENTS

There is in this subject, as in so many others, a wide divergence of views. Some feel that spiritual gifts and natural talents are one and the same. John Stott asks, "Is it not *a priori* unlikely that God will give a spiritual gift of teaching to a believer who in pre-conversion days could not teach for toffee?"[3] This is precisely what God *did* in the case of Peter. There is no evidence that he displayed the gift of teaching or evangelism before Pentecost, but he used those gifts wonderfully at Pentecost and after, as is obvious both in the Acts of the Apostles and in the letters of Peter. Moreover, countless missionaries report that such spiritual gifts are given to most unlikely people who come to the Lord out of pagan backgrounds. Neither is this experience limited to the mission field, but is often demonstrated in the homeland.

That most balanced and persuasive of Pentecostal writers, Donald Gee, has some interesting comments on this subject:

> I can remember hearing the late Smith Wigglesworth, who was an illiterate man, utter truths that went far beyond his natural capacity to comprehend or express. He could amaze trained theologians by their profundity and hold them spellbound. I am sure the preacher himself did not know the full significance of what he had said though he was conscious of words that had come in a special way by the Spirit. Other preachers have tasted the same thrilling experience.[4]

There is undoubtedly a place where natural talents and spiritual gifts overlap, but sorry indeed is the man who relies on

---

[3]Stott, *Baptism and Fullness,* p. 93.

[4]Donald Gee, *Spiritual Gifts in the Work of the Ministry Today* (Springfield, Mo.: Gospel Publishing House, 1963), pp. 29-30.

natural talent to do the Lord's work. Just as well attack a tiger tank with a can opener. One encouragement to many who are struggling is that through the gifts of the Holy Spirit he may experience God's power to undertake work for God, that by human standards he is unqualified to perform. Indeed no Christian is entitled to ask, "Am I qualified?" but only, "Is it the will of God?" If it is the will of God the Holy Spirit will be our qualification.

SPIRITUAL GIFTS AND HUMAN PERSONALITIES

A common mistake is to assume that when the Holy Spirit is ministering through the spiritual gifts of a person, his personality is somehow by-passed. This is particularly true when gifts such as the gift of tongues is being considered. In the catalog of spiritual gifts as recorded in 1 Corinthians 12:28 and 30 the New English Bible, in dealing with the gift of tongues, calls it, "the gift of ecstatic utterance of various kinds." This is a particularly unfortunate translation of these verses. It is inaccurate from the scholarly point of view, and from the practical point of view it is very misleading. A dictionary definition of ecstasy is, "a trance, especially one resulting from great religious fervor." The suggestion here is that the person does not have real control over the exercise of his spiritual gift. Paul makes it clear, however, that in the true exercise of such a gift, the person involved has real conscious control. The basic implication of 1 Corinthians 14:26-33 is that each Christian is to control the way his gift is used. Nowhere is this clearer than in verse 32: "the spirits of prophets are subject to prophets." There would be absolutely no point in Paul's giving instructions as to how the gifts of prophecy and tongues should be used, if individuals had no control over their gifts.

I have been in meetings where people seemed to be in a trance-like condition when apparently they were speaking in tongues or prophesying. I had the conviction that this was not in the power of the Spirit but rather of the flesh, or worse. However, it should not surprise us if a person ministering by one of the spiritual gifts displays some idiosyncrasies or individual characteristics. This happens continually with someone exercising the gift of teaching or evangelism. God does not obliterate personality. He refines it and uses it. Indeed, preaching has been defined as truth through personality.

It is often claimed that some of the gifts of the Spirit are psychological or even satanic in origin. It is true for example that the phenomenon of tongues is known among pagan religions, but virtually all spiritual gifts have counterfeits and this is no new occurrence. The Book of Exodus records the Dealings of God with Pharaoh through Moses. Moses performed a number of miracles in the presence of Pharaoh, and the wise men and sorcerers duplicated the first few "by their secret arts." This in no sense invalidates the miracles performed by Moses. As a very young pastor I was brought face to face with a spiritualist healer. I had no doubt that he was controlled by satanic power, but that does not mean that all healing is satanic in origin.

It is a mistake to be gullible and to think that every unusual occurrence is of God. It is probably much more serious to question the spiritual experiences of others simply because we have not had those experiences ourselves. Rather let us recognize the potential we have to serve the Lord and His church through spiritual gifts, and then let us ask the Lord to give us one or more of these gifts.

Every Christian has a gift, but let us not be satisfied with one gift. Instead, we should follow Paul's advice and "earnestly desire the higher gifts." If God does not see fit to grant us the gifts we most desire, let us be conscientious in using the gift or gifts that He has given us. Let us also be sure to rejoice in the gifts that He has given to other Christians.

FOR DISCUSSION

1. Name two problems we face in dealing with spiritual gifts.
2. Were spiritual gifts withdrawn after the apostles died? State your reasons.

3. Are all gifts from the Holy Spirit or can they be counterfeited?

4. Has the gift of teaching been abused? Name some examples.

5. If we lack a spiritual gift, what action should we take?

6. Study in detail one of the spiritual gifts that are found in the New Testament.

7. Do spiritual gifts vary in importance? Give biblical reasons.

8. Consider the relationship between spiritual gifts and natural talents. Are they the same?

9. In the exercise of a spiritual gift is the human personality involved?

14

The Gifts of the Holy Spirit and the Fruits of the Holy Spirit

There was a great tendency in the church at Corinth for the believers to be so engrossed with spiritual gifts that they paid little attention to spiritual conduct. This is still largely true today. A Christian tends to be regarded as a spiritual giant if he has a great preaching gift or has great success in evangelism. In fact, to be effective in Christian service proves little except the fact that God is able to use ordinary people in extraordinary ways. I have known men living in the sin of adultery who were still used by the Holy Spirit to bring people to faith in Jesus Christ. I once had a woman tell me bluntly that she knew she was a backslider and had little interest in the things of God but that she could still speak in tongues. I did not doubt her for a moment. For many of us preachers it is much easier to preach than to control irritability or pride.

It is not by chance that the sublime passage on love in 1 Corinthians 13 is placed exactly in the middle of the entire section dealing with spiritual gifts, between chapters 12 and 14. We have seen that Paul exhorted the Corinthians and us to "earnestly desire the higher gifts," but so far we have not emphasized the fact that the main emphasis is on the second half of that verse: "earnestly desire the higher gifts. *And I will show you a still more excellent way*" (1 Cor. 12:31, italics mine). Paul then proceeds to list seven spiritual gifts and to stress that love is more important than all of them. He begins with the gift of tongues, proceeds to the gift of prophecy, and then lists the understanding of mysteries, the gift of knowledge, of faith, generosity, and then sacrifice of possessions, and even

116

of life itself. But, he says, they are as nothing if not accompanied by the spiritual fruit of love.

> If I speak in the tongues of men and of angels, but have not love, I am a noisy gong or a clanging cymbal. And if I have prophetic powers, and understand all mysteries and all knowledge, and if I have all faith, so as to remove mountains, but have not love, I am nothing. If I give away all I have, and if I deliver my body to be burned, but have not love, I gain nothing. Love is patient and kind; love is not jealous or boastful; it is not arrogant or rude. Love does not insist on its own way; it is not irritable or resentful; it does not rejoice at wrong, but rejoices in the right. Loves bears all things, believes all things, hopes all things, endures all things. Love never ends; as for prophecies, they will pass away; as for tongues, they will cease; as for knowledge, it will pass away. For our knowledge is imperfect and our prophecy is imperfect; but when the perfect comes, the imperfect will pass away. When I was a child, I spoke like a child, I thought like a child, I reasoned like a child; when I became a man, I gave up childish ways. For now we see in a mirror dimly, but then face to face. Now I know in part; then I shall understand fully, even as I have been fully understood. So faith, hope, love abide, these three; but the greatest of these is love. Make love your aim, and earnestly desire the spiritual gifts, especially that you may prophesy (1 Cor. 13:1-14:1).

We are living in a period of history when we need to grasp anew the purpose of God for His children. It is a period of Hollywood evangelism. The only question that seems to be asked by many is, "Does it get results?" To get results, almost every exploitation of show-biz personalities and athletes, as well as dubious Madison Avenue techniques, is pressed into service.

In contrast to this common attitude is the example of Robert Murray McCheyne, the saintly Church of Scotland pastor who stressed, "The most important thing for my people is my personal holiness." I was speaking to a meeting of students some years ago and to underline this point I said, "God is more interested in what Billy Graham is than in what he does." An undergraduate from Yale hotly differed with me, and we discussed the significance of the verse, "For those whom he foreknew he also predestined to be conformed to the image of his Son, in order that he might be the first-born among many brethren" (Rom. 8:29). It is paraphrased by Phillips, "God, in his foreknowledge, chose them to bear the family likeness of his Son, that he might be the eldest of a family of many brothers." I knew that Billy Graham would be the first to emphasize this truth. Soon my undergraduate friend came to believe it also.

I used to think that the greatest miracle God could perform was to make me a preacher. After He had done so I came to realize that it required a far greater miracle to make me holy.

I remember visiting a fine missionary in Algeria whom I had met years previously in the Air Force in North Africa. He was very despondent. When I asked what the problem was, he explained that despite all his faithful work and prayer, he had had little or no response from the Muslims among whom he had worked. He said, "I cannot get away from the scripture, 'You did not choose me, but I chose you and appointed you that you should go and bear fruit and that your fruit should abide' (John 15:16). I am a fruitless Christian," he said, "because I am not winning Algerians to the Lord." We then had a talk about fruit and I reminded him about a passage in Galatians: "the fruit of the Spirit is love, joy, peace patience, kindness, goodness, faithfulness, gentleness, self-control" (Gal. 5:22-23). A fruitful Christian is not necessarily one who is seeing great results in evangelism or in any other gift, but is one who is showing forth these fruits in his life. This missionary had fallen into a common trap, as had many other Christians, and seemed relieved after we had talked about the matter.

Paul made it clear that Christians do not necessarily have all the gifts, but they should have all the fruits. The use of the word fruit is significant. Fruit is not something that can be artificially produced; we cannot go into a workshop and make a grapefruit. Fruit is a product of life, and it is only as the life-giving power of the Holy Spirit lives fully in us that genuine fruit will appear in our lives. This process of fruit-bearing also takes time. A spiritual gift may make its presence known immediately, but fruit-bearing cannot be hurried. To be sure, we can buy artificial fruit, but its artificial nature is easily detectable even before we try to eat it.

A person may have many spiritual gifts and be utterly unlike Jesus Christ. John Sung was a very effective Chinese evangelist with a wonderful experience of God's saving grace, but he had an ungovernable temper and was known to dismiss as many as three interpreters in the course of one address. The gift was great but the fruit was scarce.

When we talk about witnessing to a person we often mean verbalizing Christian truth, but witnessing really involves much more than that. We read of the early church in Jerusalem that the Christians were "praising God and having favor with all the people" (Acts 2:47). Our aim should be to please God rather than to seek worldly popularity, but it would be much easier to preach with apostolic effectiveness if the church was living in apostolic holiness. Donald Gee writes,

> Now I want to speak of those who make a big outward show of the gifts of the Spirit but seem to have very little of the fruit, very little holiness; their lives are not showing the grace of our Lord Jesus Christ. These are the people who do more harm to the Pentecostal testimony than all the writers and preachers who have written and spoken against it put together.[1]

The significance of these words is accentuated when we bear in mind that Donald Gee is the most eloquent and balanced spokesman of the Pentecostal movement, and that this was written as long ago as 1945. What he saw as a threat to the Pentecostal movement is in fact a threat to the whole Christian testimony. It was this attitude that Paul strove to correct in his first letter to the Corinthians. Gee goes on to write:

[1]Donald Gee, *Now That You've Been Baptized in the Spirit* (Springfield, Mo.: Gospel Publishing House, 1972), pp. 27-28.

The same is true with regard to people's attitude in a meeting. Some think that as long as they can preach they are right spiritually; as long as they can lead in prayer or testify, they think they are in health spiritually; they say, "Oh, I am all right! Look how I can take part in a meeting!" The test of your spiritual life is not what you are in a meeting. It is what you are when you are alone with God. Some of us love to pray in public, but do we love secret prayer? Some of us love to feel the glory and enthusiasm of a crowd, especially in a live, revival meeting, but we shrink from the Garden of Gethsemane. When in a great spiritual meeting you say, "I feel grand!" but brother, the test of your spiritual life is whether you feel grand when alone with God; when the hours spent in His presence are like heaven on earth.[2]

It should not surprise us that in the list of the works of the flesh there are at least fifteen, while the fruits of the Spirit number nine (Gal. 5:19-21). There are times when judgment has to be exercised, as when the disciples were urged to choose "seven men of good repute, full of the Spirit and of wisdom" (Acts 6:3). When such a selection is made it cannot be merely on the basis of spiritual gifts. Gifts of the Spirit do not necessarily prove that a man is Spirit-filled; in addition we have to look for evidence of spiritual fruit, for that cannot be falsified for any period of time.

FOR DISCUSSION

1. Some Christians are greatly used by God. Is this an evidence of spirituality?
2. Where does Paul list seven spiritual gifts to show that spiritual fruit is more important?
3. Is God more interested in our Christian service or in our character?
4. What is meant by spiritual fruitfulness?
5. Should Christians have *all* the spiritual gifts?
6. Should Christians have *all* the spiritual fruits?
7. What is involved in Christian witnessing?

[2]Ibid, p. 28.

15

Some Individual Spiritual Gifts

Consideration was given in chapter 13 to the subject of spiritual gifts in general. It may be helpful to consider at least some of them in more detail. There seem to be twenty gifts mentioned in the New Testament, but there is apparently some overlapping and some duplication. Although there are obviously separate gifts, to stress their differences too rigidly will obscure rather than clarify our understanding.

First, let us look at the gifts listed in 1 Corinthians 12:28-30, where we are given what seems to be a systematic, though not comprehensive, list of gifts in order of their importance. After that we shall look at other gifts mentioned elsewhere.

APOSTLES

I used to hold the widely accepted view that the number of apostles was twelve, that their qualification was that they had been witnesses of the life, death, and resurrection of our Lord, and that they were commissioned by Him. This view necessarily means that when the original twelve died the office of apostle ceased to exist. It also poses the problem of Paul, but this is generally accounted for by Paul's reference to himself: "(The Lord) appeared to Cephas, then to the twelve. Then he appeared to more than five hundred brethren at one time, most of whom are still alive, though some have fallen asleep. Then he appeared to James, then to all the apostles. Last of all, *as to one untimely born, he appeared also to me*" (1 Cor. 15:5-8, italics mine).

The actual number of twelve and the insistence that they were all men who had been with Jesus throughout His ministry comes mostly from one passage in Acts.

> "So one of the men who have accompanied us during all the time that the Lord Jesus went in and out among us, beginning from the baptism of John until the day when he was taken up from us—one of these men must become with us a witness to his resurrection." And they put forward two, Joseph called Barsabbas, who was surnamed Justus, and Matthias. And they prayed and said, "Lord, who knowest the hearts of all men, show which one of these two thou hast chosen to take the place in this ministry and apostleship from which Judas turned aside, to go to his own place." And they cast lots for them, and the lot fell on Matthias; and he was enrolled with the eleven apostles (Acts 1:21-26).

After closer investigation and thought this seems to be an inconclusive basis for a fairly important truth. Was Peter speaking with divine authority? Was the New Testament way of selecting an apostle to be determined by the casting of lots? If so, why was it not used again in the New Testament? Why do we not hear of Matthias again? Of course there were others among the Twelve who were not heard of again and the argument from silence is at best uncertain, but gathering all the available pieces of evidence it does seem slender.

Another view is that an apostle was a special messenger; and in our day this is usually interpreted as being a missionary. A wide knowledge of missionaries and their gifts makes this view hard to accept. What indeed is the definition of missionary? Perhaps the best one is a person who has crossed a cultural or geographic frontier in the service of Jesus Christ.[1]

In the New Testament the word apostle is certainly used of more than the Twelve, as witness Matthias (Acts 1:26) and James (Gal. 1:19); Barnabas and Paul seem to have been

---

[1]Today this often means being an agricultural adviser or engineer and often has little to do with the spiritual gift of apostleship.

regarded as apostles, and possibly Luke also. The word is used of our Lord, "Consider Jesus, the apostle and high priest of our confession" (Heb. 3:1). It is used also in other places as in Revelation 21:14, "And the wall of the city had twelve foundations, and on them the twelve names of the twelve apostles of the Lamb." This reference to the number of the Twelve is difficult to reconcile with the much larger number of men who were described as apostles. While we cannot necessarily explain all apparent difficulties, we accept the truth of the Scripture. In passing it should be noted that the "apostle James" mentioned in Galatians 1:19 is referred to as the brother of Christ while He was on earth. In the light of all this information the one clear fact that emerges is that there is no room for dogmatism. Godly and thoughtful men have advanced a variety of views.

Several other things seem fairly clear to me. It would seem as if Peter and Paul, and possibly others, possessed *all* the spiritual gifts. Apostles were not normally a gift to one local church but rather to the church universal. They usually traveled in a team of at least two, often more, and their ministry called them to travel through one or many countries. At times they stayed in one place for a relatively long period; Paul lived at Ephesus for two years, where he was a church planter, evangelist, teacher, pastor, etc. It seems probable that even if some apostles did not possess all the gifts, the gifts of the individuals in a team were complementary.

Many Christians are of the opinion that the apostolic gift has passed away and that there are no apostles today. For many years I subscribed to that view but now I am less convinced. Few men would have the temerity to claim that they are apostles. During my ministry, however, I have met at least some men who seem to be performing the work of an apostle, as far as is possible in the changed circumstances of the twentieth century. They are exercising a wide range of spiritual gifts in their ministry.

That there are not more apostles today may well be due to the way in which we have ordered church life and mission boards. I do not know of many missions which would accept Peter and the other apostles for the field and I know of hundreds of churches where Paul would not be invited to preach, and many more where he would not be invited back. Neither would the average church member, with his view of church government, take kindly to an apostle appointing elders as leaders of a local church. It may well be that the gift of apostleship would yet flourish if we gave the Lord more freedom to operate.

In the New and the Old Testaments the gift and office of the prophet is regarded as a particularly important one. Yet today it is another gift that causes disagreement. I believe there may be some areas of overlap between prophecy and teaching, and though I treat them separately some duplication will be inevitable.

In several places prophecy is grouped with apostleship as the first two gifts (see 1 Cor. 12:28; Eph. 4:11), and Paul writes, "Make love your aim, and earnestly desire the spiritual gifts, *especially that you may prophecy*" (1 Cor. 14:1). I have not read one writer who denies that the prophetic office was important in the early days of the church, but some believe that once the canon of Scripture had been fixed and Christians had a Bible, the need for prophecy ended. Occasionally some refer to the Scripture, "As for prophecies, they will pass away" (1 Cor. 13:8). But *when* will they pass away? The answer seems to lie in verse 10: "When the perfect comes, the imperfect will pass away." We have not yet reached the age of perfection, and many of us feel that perfection will not come until the Lord Jesus Christ returns.

There are many in our day who feel that teaching and prophecy are one and the same thing. It is difficult to reconcile that view with the situation in Antioch where both existed: "Now in the church at Antioch there were prophets and teachers" (Acts 13:1). This does not necessarily mean that apostles did not prophesy, but it certainly does imply that there was a distinction between the two ministries of teaching and prophecy.

Throughout the whole of the Old Testament, prophecy was greatly honored by God, even though the prophets themselves were often the targets of persecution. The ministry of the prophets had two main aspects and we shall look at these separately.

First was the ministry that concerned forecasting events in the future, a little like weather forecasters, but fortunately they were much more accurate!

The second function of the prophet was to speak as God's messenger concerning the present.

The Prophet As Forecaster

Many people still believe that the role of the prophet was to foretell the future and little else. This was important particularly in relation to the first coming of Christ. It should be pointed out, however, that despite all the Old Testament promises of the Incarnation, few people understood them clearly enough to expect the advent of the Messiah when He appeared. Perhaps the most important role of prophecy was to enable godly men to look back after the event had taken place and see that all the various pieces of prophecy fitted together. This not only authenticated Jesus Christ; it also proved in one way that God controlled future events, and that His word was utterly reliable. In our present age there is too great a tendency to be dogmatic concerning the second coming of our Lord. We preach, write, and make prognostications which, when not fulfilled, cause disillusionment.

In the Old Testament, foretelling occupies a much smaller place than forthtelling. The question arises whether the forecasting role of the prophet is still valid in our day.

It is recorded that in Armenia, which is mainly in Russia but partly in Turkey, an eleven-year-old boy in the village of Kara Kala received a series of prophecies in the year 1855. He foretold that the Turks would turn upon the Armenians, and warned the Christians to escape by crossing the seas. Little lasting effect was produced by these prophecies. In the year 1900 that prophet, now middle-aged, named Efim Gerasemovitch Klubniken (or Little prophet), again began to pass on to his people more warnings. In the same year a mass emigration of Pentecostals began, and continued for twelve years. In April, 1914, the Turks savagely turned upon what was left of the Armenian population and killed between 1 1/2 and 2 million of them with great brutality. The effect of the Armenian massacres was to cause a wave of revulsion to sweep through Europe. The Armenians were, and are, a highly intelligent race with a long and distinguished history going back to the Persian and Babylonian empires. The people who remained in Kara Kala were among those massacred. But thanks to the prophecy of Efim the Pentecostal families had fled for safety to many countries in the Middle East, including Lebanon, and also in Argentina, the U.S.A., etc. More details of this are given in chapter 20.

I must confess that when I first heard of this prophecy and its consequences I treated it with great caution, for it was not like anything I had heard of before. There was but one question to ask: Was it consistent with the Bible? I recalled the story of Agabus in Acts 11:27-28: "Now in these days prophets came down from Jerusalem to Antioch. And one of them named Agabus stood up and foretold by the Spirit that there would be a great famine over all the world; and this took place in the days of Claudius." No amount of careful Bible teaching could have brought such a direct message from God. Then there was the prophecy of our Lord to Peter in John 21:18-19. " 'Truly, truly, I say to you, when you were young, you girded yourself and walked where you would; but when you are old, you will stretch out your hands, and another will gird you and carry you where you do not wish to go.' (This he said to show by what death he was to glorify God.)" There is a strong historical probability that this was literally fulfilled.

One other important illustration is that of Jesus when He prophesied concerning Jerusalem: "So when you see the desolating sacrilege spoken of by the prophet Daniel, standing in the holy place (let the reader understand), then let those who are in Judea flee to the mountains; let him who is on the housetop not go down to take what is in his house; and let him who is in the field not turn back to take his mantle. And alas for those who are with child and for those who give suck in those days! Pray that your flight may not be in winter or on a sabbath. For then there will be great tribulation, such as has not been from the beginning of the world until now, no, and never will be. And if those days had not been shortened, no human being would be saved; but for the sake of the elect those days will be shortened" (Matt. 24:15-22). In part, this refers to the destruction of Jerusalem that had taken place in 170 B.C. in the reign of Antiochus Epiphanes, who desecrated the altar by sacrificing pigs' flesh upon it. Jesus also looks forward to the future and forecasts that Jerusalem will again be the scene of terrible suffering. There is room for differing views concerning this passage and the second coming of Christ, but what is important for our purpose is to report that approximately forty years after Christ uttered these words the Roman legions (or eagles) under the command of Titus laid siege to the city (in A.D. 70). The Christians, having been forewarned by the prophecy, escaped from Jerusalem, crossed the river Jordan, and made their way to safety in the town of Pella. In so doing they missed one of the most ghastly sieges in history. According to Josephus, 1,100,000 died under the most horrible conditions and a further 97,000 were taken prisoner. Paul received a prophecy in Acts 21:4, but ignored it and decided to go to Jerusalem even though it resulted in his imprisonment.

The Prophet As a Forthteller

In grouping these accounts of the foretelling aspect of prophecy it is dangerously possible to give the impression that the principal task of the prophet is to forecast. In the Scripture as a whole the prophet was far more often entrusted to give a message of warning or encouragement with God's authority. One example is that of Nathan, who denounced the sin of King David in 2 Samuel 12:1-18. This led David to write his great psalm of repentance, Psalm 51.

Paul instructs in 1 Corinthians 14:29, "Let two or three prophets speak, and let the others weigh what is said." This is not likely to mean that two or three prophets would give prophecies concerning the future in the way that has been discussed. I still view forecasting with caution, but do not consider it impossible. When I have heard any kind of prophecy I have been eager to talk to other witnesses whose judgment I respect and "weigh what is said." Most times there has been a remarkable degree of unanimity as to whether it was "in the flesh" or "in the Spirit." There have been times when the message has been much in tune with the whole spirit of the meeting, and others when it seemed to jar. All too often it has been a collection of clichés bellowed out in King James English.

I remember preaching at a large charismatic church. After the sermon a woman made her way to the microphone, the organist began to play, and the woman sang a solo that was marvelously appropriate. Later I learned that not only had it not been planned, and the organist not informed, but the singer was a godly woman who never normally sang solos. On the best of occasions when a prophecy has been given in an orderly way, and with a minimum of fuss, I have been inclined to think it much like what would take place at a good meeting of the Christian Brethren.

Michael Green has this to say about prophecy:

> One commonly hears it said that prophecy is the same as preaching or teaching. This could only be maintained in defiance of the whole weight of New Testament evidence. . . . It is one thing to prepare one's address in dependence on the Spirit, and to preach it in the power of that same Spirit; it is quite another thing to find the Spirit taking over and speaking directly

from Christ through you, in words that you had never intended to use at all.[2]

I am not acquainted with Michael Green, but this quote has the ring of experience to it. Although I am not always enthusiastic about what passes as prophecy in charismatic churches, I believe that one of the many things we need to hear today is the authentic prophetic note sounded from our pulpits. While agreeing with what Michael Green has written, it will be necessary to avoid too great a distinction between prophecy and teaching, as we shall see as we deal with our next gift.

In chapter 8, on the Holy Spirit and Pentecost, we noticed that a characteristic of apostolic preaching was authority. The same characteristic was notable in the earthly ministry of Jesus Christ: "And when Jesus finished these sayings, the crowds were astonished at his teaching, for he taught them as one who had authority, and not as their scribes" (Matt. 7:28-29).

This note of authority was certainly obvious in the ministry of Paul, as well as Peter, and in both the Old and New Testaments prophets this quality was striking. Perhaps we should pay much more attention to praying for the genuine prophetic note of authority to be heard in our day in place of the usual pablum.

The prophets were not often popular. The very authority of their preaching often made them difficult to live with. Because they were the mouthpieces of God, there was often a cutting edge to their statements that was directed at those with whom God was displeased.

TEACHERS

Teaching has a very important place in the New Testament. This makes it all the more baffling that so few really good Bible

---

[2]Michael Green, *I Believe in the Holy Spirit* (Grand Rapids: Eerdmans, 1975), p. 171. Used by permission.

teachers are found in ordinary church life, and that congregations are so slow to encourage the gift when they can. Not merely is teaching the next gift mentioned in 1 Corinthians 12:28, but it also played a large part in the early ministry of our Lord. He made it part of His great commission: "Go therefore and make disciples of all nations, baptizing them in the name of the Father and of the Son and of the Holy Spirit, *teaching them to observe all that I have commanded you*" (Matt. 28:19-20, italics mine). It occurs repeatedly in the early chapters of Acts: "they devoted themselves to the apostles' teaching" (Acts 2:42). In fact, it could be described as a teaching and a learning church. The gift is also mentioned in Romans 12:7 and Ephesians 4:11.

I remember talking to an American Episcopalian pastor who had received "the baptism and the fullness of the Spirit" simultaneously, some years after he had been ordained. One day when we were seated in a coffee shop, I asked him what he felt was his strongest gift or gifts. He replied, "I have always felt that it was pastoral visitation, but since I have come into blessing I have discovered that I must also teach." There was a pause, and then he added, "I have found that teaching is really hard work." His reply brings us to the heart of the matter. Good teaching requires hard work and lots of it. I am constantly appalled when I visit pastors in their offices. Almost always that is what they are, "offices," when they should be studies. Jowett, the great British preacher, once said, "If the study is a lounge the pulpit is an impertinence." A poor library makes for poor preaching.

Teaching requires great sacrifice. To obtain an adequate library is very expensive and to move it means much greater expense. It also requires great self-discipline to make study the first priority. In these days the average pastor finds that he is swamped with counseling and administration. The church members who are largely responsible for this state of affairs are doing an immense disservice to themselves and to their pastors. Surely, one day these people will have to account for the way in which they have squandered the time and energy of highly trained men who are compelled to spend most of their time in numerous committees and office work. I shall never cease to be grateful that after my ordination the Lord led me to a quiet country pastorate where the people gave me *time* to study and God gave me the *desire,* although it still required a lot of self-discipline. No amount of academic training can take the place of daily study. For those who do not have this gift I am convinced that the way to begin is to "seek earnestly the gift," and then ruthlessly lay aside the inevitable distractions.

Sermonettes produce Christianettes. To take profound truth and to make it simple is the difficult but glorious calling of all pastors and teachers. Much more could be written about this subject, on which I have strong convictions, but we must not be distracted from our purpose of considering teaching as a gift of the Holy Spirit.

At the beginning of this chapter I suggested that there is probably some overlap in certain of the gifts. I believe this to be the case with prophecy and teaching. Although I have a high regard for the teaching role I believe that there are some who are rightly regarded as exceptionally good Bible teachers, but who place so much emphasis on the teaching gift that one listens in vain for some prophetic note to be sounded. For these as for others the Scripture is appropriate, "Desire the spiritual gifts, *especially that you may prophesy*" (1 Cor. 14:1, italics mine).

Soon after my ordination I became aware that it is dangerously possible to "lift" sermons from books without much difficulty. In many cases the end product would be stale and lacking in real life and power. In an attempt to avoid this I developed a settled policy for which I have been grateful ever since. I had to prepare three sermons a week. I worked very conscientiously in my preparation. If by Friday evening I had not been able to decide what I should preach on Sunday morning or evening I gave up preparation and told the Lord that I had worked hard, that I would not dare preach a "synthetic" sermon, and that I would trust the Holy Spirit to undertake. Usually on Saturday a whole address complete with subheadings and illustrations would come to mind in the space of half an hour, compared with the two or three days I would normally expect to spend in preparation. On rare occasions I did not know what I was going to preach until the service started; always I held myself open to change my subject if I judged that that was the will of God. I am not necessarily advocating this for others, but it was profitable for me. On these occasions I would often experience remarkable freedom and authority. Looking back I think this may have led to some prophetic note in what would otherwise have been simply a teaching ministry.

Many years later I was talking to one of the leaders of the Assemblies of God in the U.S.A., and I asked him how he viewed the prophetic gift. He replied that occasionally when he was preaching a well-prepared message he would experience a release of power and authority, and often he then discarded his sermon notes. He believed that this was how the prophetic gift often operated.

I believe I witnessed something of this when Melvin Hodges of the Assemblies of God was reading a paper to a group of missionary leaders. Suddenly a new vitality came into his voice, and there was a freedom and authority noticeable to all his hearers.

A word of warning needs to be introduced here. I have met several charismatic speakers who believe that after they have been "filled with the Holy Spirit" they no longer need to spend time in sermon preparation. This is an almost inevitable reaction to the years when every sermon had to be elaborately prepared, and the delivery consisted of reading it from a written manuscript. However understandable this reaction may be, shallowness is its inevitable result and the flock will be spiritually starved. Perhaps the best antidote to this tendency is to make a thorough study of the pastoral Epistles. Here we see how anxious Paul was to have the parchments, and we note his instruction to Timothy: "When you come, bring the cloak that I left with Carpus at Troas, *also the books, and above all the parchments*" (2 Tim. 4:13, italics mine).[3]

In considering prophecy and teaching it may be helpful to note that the Assemblies of God, in their Central American work, have a category for men who are not yet teachers or prophets. It applies to a person who can give a brief message of encouragement or challenge; they call such a person "an exhorter." We could do worse than to follow their example.

I touch on this subject here because although it does not appear in the catalog of spiritual gifts in 1 Corinthians 12 and 14, it is so closely related to prophecy and teaching. The gift of exhortation is mentioned in Romans 12:6-8, "Having gifts that differ according to the grace given to us, let us use them: if prophecy, in proportion to our faith; if service, in our serving; he who teaches, in his teaching; *he who exhorts, in his exhortation;* he who contributes, in liberality; he who gives aid, with zeal; he who does acts of mercy, with cheerfulness."

There are many in our churches who cannot teach or prophecy but who can give a brief exhortation. This is often the way a young person begins to minister, and if our church program allows no opportunity for this it is much poorer. How thrilling it is to hear a man, often a recent convert, pass on some spiritual thought that the Holy Spirit has given him. What he lacks in polish is often made up for by his obvious freshness and sincerity.

MIRACLE WORKERS

When thinking of miracles people usually call to mind cases of healing or of casting out of demons. However, these are separate gifts and will be dealt with individually. There are not many authenticated miracles in the writing of the Pentecostals, apart from healing and exorcism. Dennis J. Bennett has written a little on the gift of miracle working but Michael Green de-

---

[3]It is a good motto, "To prepare as if there were no Holy Spirit and to preach as if there were no preparation."

scribes him as "theologically unreliable." Judging by Bennett's treatment of the miracles in the Gospels, that description is unfortunately justified. He writes that "Jesus' miracles were performed primarily out of His compassion to meet human needs, and for practical purposes."[4]

Our Lord was approximately thirty years of age when He performed His first miracle. Does Bennett mean that Jesus felt no compassion during those first thirty years of His life? The principal purpose of Jesus' miracles is given in the passage of Scripture quoted by Bennett: "This beginning of miracles did Jesus in Cana of Galilee, *and manifested forth his glory; and his disciples believed on him*" (John 2:11 KJV, italics mine). It is important to notice that the RSV and the NEB substitute the word "sign" for miracle. Jesus Christ's miracles undoubtedly revealed His compassion, but it is much more important to know that they reveal His deity. John's Gospel was written long after the others, and he is always careful to stress the word "signs." To misunderstand this is to misunderstand the whole reason for miracles.

The word "miracles" in the phrase "then workers of miracles" (1 Cor. 12:28), is in itself something of a problem. Many scholars believe that the phrase would be better translated "the effects of power," and J. B. Phillips translates it, "He has appointed workers of spiritual power." This leaves it open for a wider interpretation, such as the casting out of demons. This is certainly miraculous, but does not appear in any of the catalogs of the spiritual gifts. We must be clear on this point. I do not doubt the ability of Jesus Christ to perform miracles. He could and did perform them in His early life, as when He calmed the storm. There are also cases of miracles that took place in the apostolic church. Two examples that come to mind are the release of Peter from prison (Acts 12:6-11), and the raising of Dorcas from the dead (Acts 9:36-42).

It is vital to see the difference between miracles and miracle

---

[4]Dennis and Rita Bennett, *The Holy Spirit and You* (Plainfield, N.J.: Logos International, 1971), p. 126.

workers. Many of us have had experiences when God has helped us in a remarkable way; and some people would call these events miracles. Regeneration is itself a miracle. We shall see later that there is such a thing as miraculous healing. What we are considering is "workers of miracles" as a different gift from "healers."

The Holy Spirit can still perform miracles and we must never forget that. But this does not necessarily mean that He *is* performing miracles today, apart from healing and exorcism. In the absence of definitive teaching and evidence we shall do well to keep an open mind and not limit God, but at the same time try to avoid gullibility and sensationalism. Certainly in the New Testament people never advertised that miracle meetings would be held.

HEALERS

Healing is a wonderful gift to the church, but its misunderstanding and abuse have caused untold misery. Sometimes it is called "faith healing," but this is neither scriptural nor correct. It puts the emphasis or the onus on the individual concerned rather than upon the Lord Himself.

Some people have been told that the reason they have not been healed is due to their lack of faith or unconfessed sin. This may be said sincerely, but it is a cruel and terrible thing to say to those who are ill. Another expression used is that of "divine healing," but this tends to obscure the fact that if healing is accomplished through conventional medicine, it is still God who does the healing. As one Christian doctor stated, "I put on the bandages but only God can heal." The most suitable and accurate term is "miraculous healing." This distinguishes healing from orthodox medicine, and places the emphasis where it belongs—on the Holy Spirit Himself.

In addition to the fact that healing is mentioned in the list of gifts in 1 Corinthians 12:28, there are of course numerous narratives that tell of healings in the apostolic church. Although Peter and Paul were used in a wonderful way in the healing of individuals, it must be stressed that healing occupied much less of their time than did teaching. It was never meant to overshadow the teaching and preaching, which took precedence over everything else in their ministry. It is always unfortunate when healing takes the central place in anyone's ministry. It is for a purpose that in this passage in 1 Corinthians, which sets the gifts in order of priority, the gift of healing is placed *after* prophecy and teaching.

I have no question that the gift of healing is legitimate. The Bible teaches that it is and there are many authenticated instances in our own time.

I had a strange experience in the early days of my ministry. A little girl who attended the church Sunday school was knocked down by a motorcycle and suffered serious injuries, including a fractured skull. Normally it was my custom in such a situation to pray for the sick person and family, but to pray in such a way that healing or otherwise was the prerogative of the God of all comfort. This time, as I led the congregation in prayer, I unexpectedly found an authority and freedom in my praying. I felt that it was right to pray definitely for healing, and that all would know it was the power of God that had brought it about.

After the service one of the church members, who was head nurse in the hospital's pediatric ward, took me aside and explained that the child's brain had suffered irreparable damage, and that if she lived she would be a vegetable. I explained that my action had been out of character and was unpremeditated, although I was quite conscious of what I was doing. Within weeks the child recovered and was normal and returned to school and Sunday school. I have never felt that I have a "gift" of healing, although I have often responded to requests to pray for the sick according to the Scripture, "Is any among you sick? Let him call for the elders of the church, and let them pray over him, anointing him with oil in the name of the Lord; and the prayer of faith will save the sick man, and the Lord will raise him up; and if he has committed sins, he will be forgiven"

(James 5:14-15). And often people have been healed in response to prayer and the laying on of hands.

There are too many well-authenticated cases of miraculous healing known to me personally and by report, for me to doubt that the Lord still heals today—but not always. It is important to remember that although Paul healed others he could not heal himself:

> And to keep me from being too elated by the abundance of revelations, a thorn was given me in the flesh, a messenger of Satan, to harass me, to keep me from being too elated. Three times I besought the Lord about this, that it should leave me; but he said to me, "My grace is sufficient for you, for my power is made perfect in weakness." I will all the more gladly boast of my weaknesses, that the power of Christ may rest upon me. For the sake of Christ, then, I am content with weaknesses, insults, hardships, persecutions, and calamities; for when I am weak, then I am strong (2 Cor. 12:7-10).

Moreover, he was not always able to heal others: "Trophimus I left ill at Miletus" (2 Tim. 4:20). It is sometimes God's will that a person's illness should take its full course or even that he should die. We do not know all His reasons for withholding healing, but often the sufferer and those around him learn through the illness and are drawn closer to Him. Some need an experience of physical suffering to enable them to be more sympathetic to others, some to slow them down and give them a chance to think, and to be alone with Him. And some are taught patience through illness. Some will cite cases where a person with a healing gift has prayed for a sick person and no healing has taken place, and then claim that the healer is a fraud. They rarely apply the same test to an evangelist! However gifted an evangelist is, there will be many who hear him but who never accept Jesus as Lord and Savior. That does not invalidate the gift. It merely stresses that in every case we are dependent on the sovereign will of God, and do not necessarily know why He at times refuses our prayers. This is true whether we pray for healing or for conversion. Not all who heard Jesus responded to Him.

There are some Christians who insist that there is healing in the atonement of Christ. I have never seen any convincing biblical evidence for this assertion. It not only seems to be unbiblical but also unreasonable. If taken to its logical conclusion it would mean that a Christian would never die.

HELPERS

The word translated "helpers" in 1 Corinthians 12:28 occurs nowhere else in the New Testament. The fact that it is so little used has led to what amounts to "educated guesses" on the part of scholars. I have always been delighted that it is included in the list, because down through the centuries the church has received untold help through unknown but conscientious people who can correctly be described as "helpers."

Many of us who have been called to public positions in the service of Jesus Christ know that our ministry is dependent to a large degree upon those who are called to be "helpers." Inevitably I think of wives whose work and sacrifice alone has made it possible for their husbands to exercise a wide public ministry. Occasionally I have been asked how it is possible for one man to attend to correspondence, sit on committees, have a counseling ministry, write books and articles, and in addition to all this engage in public speaking. The answer is that many such people have helpers who support them, and who alone make it possible for such a ministry to be performed. I write as one whose wife has sacrificially and unselfishly helped me in every phase of my ministry, and I also have enjoyed the skillful, laborious help of secretaries who could have earned much more money in secular businesses, but who have deliberately devoted themselves to the Lord's work. Not only are such helpers unknown to the public, but in many cases they get little appreciation or recognition from those for whom they work.

The majority who write on this subject suggest that the work of a helper does not call for any particular qualification by the

Holy Spirit, but this attitude seems to me to violate the whole thrust of 1 Corinthians 12, where Paul stresses that *all* gifts are from the Holy Spirit, and all are for the common good. We read about the Holy Spirit providing for the ministry of "helps" as early as Exodus.

> The LORD said to Moses, "See I have called by name Bezalel son of Uri, son of Hur, of the tribe of Judah: and I have filled him with the Spirit of God, with ability and intelligence, with knowledge and all craftmanship, to devise artistic designs, to work in gold, silver, and bronze, in cutting stones for setting, and in carving wood, for work in every craft (Exod. 31:1-5).

From this passage it is clear that the skills of wood carving, working in gold, etc. were derived directly from the Holy Spirit. By this endowed skill Bezalel was able to fulfill God's instructions for the building of the tabernacle. I believe that this point needs to be stressed. Typing can be as spiritual as preaching, and the person who feels that God has called him to these ministries can expect the Holy Spirit's help just as much as can the evangelist or teacher.

It is interesting to note that Demos Shakarian, the founder of the Full Gospel Businessmens' Fellowship, insists that he has no gift of speaking or healing, but believes his gift is that of "helps."

ADMINISTRATORS

The word "administrators" in the RSV is translated "power to guide," in the NEB. The two are not mutually exclusive. Leon Morris writes that it "denotes the activity of the steersman of a ship, the man who pilots his vessel through shoals and brings her safe to port."[5]

The guiding and governing of the churches was and often is a demanding and thankless task, and many who hold the

---

[5]Leon Morris, *Commentary on First Corinthians* (London: Tyndale Press, 1958), p. 179.

office do not necessarily possess the requisite gift. Such a ministry demands the ability to encourage and to exercise sound judgment (especially difficult when it involves personalities), and the willingness to rebuke with love when that is called for. "Let the elders who rule well be considered worthy of double honor, *especially those who labor in preaching and teaching;* for the scripture says, 'You shall not muzzle an ox when it is treading out the grain,' and, 'The laborer deserves his wages'" (1 Tim. 5:17-18, italics mine). From this passage it is obvious that there are elders who teach, and elders who do not. Probably the Presbyterians come closest to this with their distinction between "teaching elders" and "ruling elders." Where the RSV writes of double honor, the NEB translates it, "Elders who do well as leaders should be reckoned worthy of a double stipend, in particular those who labor at preaching and teaching." The context supports the interpretation of the NEB—a practice certainly not carried out by most mission boards.

It is a consolation to recognize the fact that what is required is not mainly business talents, but a qualification that comes as a gift of the Spirit. I have known of missionaries who did not have the gift of winning people to Christ but who were wonderfully gifted as administrators. They helped organize those who did have the gift of evangelism, and by working closely with them led thousands to Christ.

TONGUES

No subject has aroused more violent disagreement, or more extreme statements for and against, than the "gift of tongues." This is the phenomenon of a person's speaking a language that he or she has never learned. At the one extreme there are many who say that tongues is the sign of having received the fullness of the Spirit, and that if you have not spoken in tongues you are not "Spirit-filled." This view is stated most clearly by the Assemblies of God, and an Assemblies pastor who deviates from this view is dismissed from the denomination. At the other extreme are those who believe that speaking in tongues is a fraud or a delusion, or even that it originates from the devil. In many churches you are not allowed to preach if you *have* spoken in tongues; in others you may not if you have *not* spoken in tongues.

There have been many well-authenticated cases of tongues speaking. This sometimes occurs in a language known to others but not to the person speaking, and there are also many cases in which the language is altogether unknown.

First, it will be well to examine some biblical examples and teaching.

Tongues As an Evidence of Spirit Baptism

In the New Testament there are three clear cases where "baptism in the Spirit" was accompanied by speaking in tongues.

The first case, that of Pentecost, we examined in the chapter "The Holy Spirit at Pentecost." On this occasion tongues was one of the signs given to impress the Jewish nation that a totally new period had been ushered in by God.

The second case was at Caesarea:

> While Peter was still saying this, the Holy Spirit fell on all who heard the word. And the believers from among the circumcised who came with Peter were amazed, because the gift of the Holy Spirit had been poured out even on the Gentiles. For they heard them speaking in tongues and extolling God. Then Peter declared, "Can any one forbid water for baptizing these people who have received the Holy Spirit just as we have?" And he commanded them to be baptized in the name of Jesus Christ. Then they asked him to remain for some days (Acts 10:44-48).

The whole chapter reveals the reluctance of the Jews to accept the fact that the blessings inaugurated at Pentecost were intended for Gentiles as well as for Jews. The gift of tongues given to Cornelius and other Gentiles was effective evidence not only to Peter, but also to the skeptical church at Jerusalem.

141

"When they heard this they were silenced. And they glorified God, saying, 'Then to the Gentiles also God has granted repentance unto life'" (Acts 11:18). It is hard to conceive what other evidence God could have given that would have convinced the Jews of such a dramatic and drastic departure from normal Jewish practices and history.

The third instance occurred when Paul visited Ephesus:

> Paul passed through the upper country and came to Ephesus. There he found some disciples. And he said to them, "Did you receive the Holy Spirit when you believed?" And they said, "No, we have never even heard that there is a Holy Spirit." And he said, "Into what then were you baptized?" They said, "Into John's baptism." And Paul said, "John baptized with the baptism of repentance, telling the people to believe in the one who was to come after him, that is, Jesus." On hearing this, they were baptized in the name of the Lord Jesus. And when Paul had laid his hands upon them, the Holy Spirit came on them; and they spoke with tongues and prophesied (Acts 19:1-6).

This group of disciples had received the baptism of John the Baptist. But they had heard nothing about the glorious fact that on the basis of Christ's death and triumphal resurrection it was possible to be baptized by the Spirit, and to enjoy His continued presence. In other words, they were unconverted. When they responded to the emancipating teaching of Paul, the Holy Spirit came on them and they spoke with tongues and prophesied.

In contrast to these three occasions when tongues accompanied the "baptism of the Holy Spirit," there are many more where there is no record of tongues speaking when people received the Holy Spirit. The first of these was as early as the day of Pentecost when 3,000 were added to the church. "So those who received his word were baptized, and there were added that day about three thousand souls" (Acts 2:41). There is no mention of tongues here, as there had been in the case of the 120 at the beginning of the chapter.

Similarly in Acts 4:4 there is no mention of the converted speaking in tongues. "But many of those who heard the word believed; and the number of the men came to about five thousand." The same is true of the apostle Paul and his conversion: "So Ananias departed and entered the house. And laying his hands on him he said, 'Brother Saul, the Lord Jesus who appeared to you on the road by which you came, has sent me that you may regain your sight and be filled with the Holy Spirit.' And immediately something like scales fell from his eyes and he regained his sight. Then he rose and was baptized, and took food and was strengthened" (Acts 9:17-19). There is no mention that Paul spoke in tongues at that time. In his letter to the Corinthians he mentioned that he spoke in tongues, but he did not state that he did so at the time of his conversion, or that it was a sign of spiritual fullness.

In the first city Paul visited in Europe, he had the dramatic experience of being beaten and put in prison. An earthquake struck and the hard-boiled Roman jailer "was baptized at once, with all his family" (Acts 16:33). This of course was water baptism. There is no mention of tongues here, nor in Paul's letter to the Philippians.

At Athens Paul preached in the synagogue, the market place, and the Areopagus. We read that "some men joined him and believed" (Acts 17:34). Again there is no mention that they spoke in tongues.

In Acts 19 there is a record of Paul's visit to Ephesus. It is remarkable in that he probably spent more time there than in any other city, excepting Rome, and he taught daily for more than two years. There is a record of the response to his ministry:

This continued for two years, so that all the residents of Asia heard the word of the Lord, both Jews and Greeks. And God did extraordinary miracles by the hands of Paul, so that handkerchiefs or aprons were carried away from his body to the sick, and diseases left them and the evil spirits came out of them. Then some of the itinerant Jewish exorcists undertook to pronounce the name of the Lord Jesus over those who had evil spirits, saying, "I adjure you by the Jesus whom Paul preaches." Seven sons of a Jewish high priest named Sceva were doing this. But the evil spirit answered them, "Jesus I know, and Paul I know; but who are you?" And the man in whom the evil spirit was leaped on them, mastered all of them, and overpowered them, so that they fled out of that house naked and wounded. And this became known to all residents of Ephesus, both Jews and Greeks; and fear fell upon them all; and the name of the Lord Jesus was extolled. Many also of those who were now believers came, confessing and divulging their practices. And a number of those who practiced magic arts brought their books together and burned them in the sight of all; and they counted the value of them and found it came to fifty thousand pieces of silver. So the word of the Lord grew and prevailed mightily (Acts 19:10-20).

Again there is no mention of tongues either in this narrative, or in Paul's letter to the Ephesians in which he devotes an important section to spiritual gifts.

It would be possible to pile up more illustrations but surely they are unnecessary. I have devoted much space to this subject because I believe that the suggestion that a person is not filled with the Spirit because he has not spoken in tongues, is one of the more unfortunate errors of some charismatics. It has led to excesses and much heartache. Many sincere and godly people have suffered tortures of self-recrimination because through this erroneous teaching they have falsely believed that they have missed God's best. Some sincere and godly people have suffered greatly through the belief that they are resisting God's Spirit simply because they have not been given the gift of tongues. As Paul asks, "Are all apostles? Are all prophets? . . . Do all speak with tongues?" (1 Cor. 12:28-30).

If a person truly believes that people who have not spoken in tongues are not "spirit filled," it inevitably means that he will go to almost any length to induce speaking in tongues. Since tongues speaking is not confined to Christianity, but has been observed in paganism and Islam and even induced in unbelievers by psychologists, it is obvious that such extreme attempts are fraught with great danger.

Don Basham quotes with great approval Derek Prince's response to the question, " 'Can you have the Baptism in the Holy Spirit without speaking in tongues?' I like Rev. Derek Prince's response to that question. He answers with another question: 'Can an elephant be an elephant without a trunk?' The answer is, 'Yes, but a trunkless elephant is a pretty funny-looking elephant.' " Basham so approves of this metaphor that he mentions "trunkless elephants" several times. Perhaps this could be regarded as humorous, if somewhat childish, if it was not followed by advice on how to "receive the baptism." Here is an extract from his book; an actual transcription of instructions that Don Basham reports he has used with numerous groups.

> Now the first thing I want to tell you is this: You can sit back and relax, for you *can* receive the baptism in the Holy Spirit and you *can* speak in tongues. It is in your power to do all you have to do. The same faith that enabled you to receive Jesus Christ as your Saviour is all the faith you need to receive the baptism in the Holy Spirit with speaking in tongues. After all, the baptism, in one sense, is simply receiving more of Jesus. It's meeting Him in a new dimension, as the Baptizer in the Holy Spirit as John the Baptist spoke of Him in Luke 3:16. There is no reason why everyone of you . . . will not receive the Holy Spirit and be praising God in a new and unknown tongue within a very few minutes. So relax and be confident. It will happen.
>
> I want to take a few minutes to explain the procedure we are going to follow . . . . The first step is receiving the Holy Spirit within; the second is to manifest the Spirit's presence by praising God in a new or "unknown" tongue. Again, let me make it clear; *everyone of you can do this.* It is within your power, once you understand what is required of you, to receive the Holy Spirit and to speak in tongues.
>
> Now when the prayer for you to receive is offered (and I'm simply going to pray one single prayer aloud in behalf of all of you, asking the Lord Jesus to baptize you in the Holy Spirit and to enable you to praise Him in a new, supernatural way), im-

mediately after the ending of that prayer, I will ask you to do a very simple thing. I will ask you to open your mouth and breathe in or drink in a deep, full breath of air. . . .

All right. That's the first step; "breathing in" the Holy Spirit and having faith that He's coming in. And that is the easiest of the two steps. But we don't want to stop there; we also want you to have the Scriptural confirmation of the Holy Spirit's presence in your life in a new way by having you receive the manifestation of speaking in tongues. Again, let me tell you, relax! You *can* do this. You *can* receive the evidence of speaking in tongues. It is in your power to do it. Let me explain what I mean.

Speaking in tongues—which is the scriptural proof or sign that you have received the baptism in the Holy Spirit—is a miracle; it is supernatural. I believe we are all agreed on that. But let me remind you again that miracles are comprised of two parts; man's part (which is natural) and God's part (which is supernatural). One of the best Scriptural examples of this truth is the miracle of Peter's walking on the water, recorded in Matthew 14. You remember the story. . . .

So when the time comes for you to speak in tongues, be ready! After I have prayed the prayer in your behalf, and immediately after you have opened your mouth and breathed in the Holy Spirit, I'm going to tell you to let that breath out. Only, do not let it out silently; but put the sound of your voice behind it. Just begin to praise God with the sound of your voice as if you never learned the English language. God already knows you can speak English, so don't even attempt to praise Him in your natural language. If you start to pray or praise in English, you'll only have to stop before you can begin to speak in tongues. Even the Holy Spirit cannot make you speak two languages at once. . . .

Now when I give the word for you to open your mouth and begin to praise God, I know from experience that some of you will receive tongues instantly. Others of you will be a little hesitant to begin to speak. But just gather your courage and begin to speak anyway. Just babble out whatever pops into your mind or whatever you feel on your lips and tongue. And once you begin, keep it up. Don't stop. Let the language flow out freely. If you can speak five words or syllables, you can speak five thousand. The Holy Spirit has an unlimited vocabulary.

146

And another thing. When you start to speak, don't worry about what it sounds like. It may sound like Chinese, like Polynesian, like the notes of the musical scale, or even like baby-talk. What it sounds like is the Holy Spirit's business. Your business is just to speak out. The Holy Spirit will give you words and syllables in the language He wants you to pray in. Don't get concerned if the person sitting next to you is praying with different sounds from yours. Don't examine it, just do it! . . .

Now, I believe it's time to pray. Relax, and get ready for what is going to happen. You are about to move into a deep and wonderful new dimension of Christian experience, even though it happens in what may seem to be a strange and foolish way. Never mind. It's real. It's supernatural. And believe me, after today, your life will never be the same! Let's pray.

Dear Jesus, we thank you for the promise of your Holy Spirit today. We thank you that you are pouring out your Holy Spirit with the blessing of speaking in tongues. Lord, we ask you to honor the faith of all the people in this room, and to confirm your word in them. We ask you right now, Lord Jesus, to baptize everyone in this room with your Holy Spirit, and enable them to praise you with a language they never learned but which is pleasing to you. Thank you, Lord Jesus, Amen.

Now, every one of you, "Receive ye the Holy Ghost" and praise God in other tongues! Amen!

All right, open your mouth and take in that deep breath of air. Breathe in deeply and as you do, believe the Holy Spirit is coming in. That's right! Good!

Now, let that breath out, and begin to praise God with the sound of your voice, and receive the utterance the Holy Spirit gives![6]

I am convinced that Mr. Basham is sincerely anxious to give the greatest possible help that he can to people, and that his motives are absolutely pure. I am equally convinced that what he has written and apparently continues to practice is psychological manipulation, rather than Christian teaching. It just will not do. It is neither scriptural nor sensible. It has been

[6]Don W. Basham, *Ministering the Baptism in the Holy Spirit* (Springdale, Pa.: Whitaker House, 1971), pp. 54-64.

my responsibility to try to undo the damage caused by this type of approach.

That the gift of tongues can be a real blessing I do not deny, but it is clearly taught that it is the least important of the spiritual gifts. It is a great mistake when it is allowed to dominate every other spiritual gift and ministry.

There are some who deny that in the list of gifts given in 1 Corinthians 12:28-30 a priority of importance is intended, but that seems an impossible view for two reasons. First, the list is clearly stated numerically; for example, first apostles, second prophets, third teachers, and so on. Second, Paul urges Christians to "earnestly desire the higher gifts" (1 Cor. 12:31). How can we know what are those "higher gifts" unless Paul has indicated an order of importance?

To take any truth and to overemphasize it is to create a caricature rather than a portrait. In the history of the Church that is precisely how most heresies began. It is especially serious when the point that is overstressed is of relatively minor importance.

Is Tongues Speaking for Today?

My first serious encounter with tongues speaking occurred thirty years ago, when a member of the church that I pastored plunged into an extreme form of Pentecostalism. I studied the subject thoroughly to decide what my attitude should be. I could not escape Paul's instruction, "*do not forbid speaking in tongues; but all things should be done decently and in order*" (1 Cor. 14:39-40, italics mine). I still cannot ignore that command.

Later I was impressed by the fact that when Paul was stressing the importance of prophecy he also said, "I thank God that I speak in tongues more than you all" (1 Cor. 14:18). I obviously could not condemn a gift that Paul thanked God for, nor could I disregard his words, "*Now I want you all to speak in tongues, but even more to prophesy*" (1 Cor. 14:5, italics mine). Obviously he regards prophecy as more important than

148

tongues, but that does not invalidate the first half of the verse.

Much later I heard many godly people speak in tongues, in a wide variety of countries and in differing situations. In addition I read many carefully authenticated cases of tongues speaking. To deny its validity would have been to accuse thousands of sincere people of being out of line with God's will. Should a person do this simply because he has not experienced the gift himself? The idea is unthinkable.

What Help Is the Gift of Tongues?

As stressed in the chapter on Pentecost, the gift of tongues was not necessary at Pentecost for communication, and neither is that the purpose of the gift today. There is a good deal of debate as to whether the gift of tongues is an actual language, or whether it is simply a collection of sounds of supernatural origin. There have been well-authenticated cases where people have recognized a known language even when the speaker did not know that he was speaking in a known tongue.

John Sherrill recorded a number of different individuals speaking in tongues, and invited six linguists to examine them. They could not identify by name any of the languages; he had skillfully slipped onto the tapes two instances of pure made-up gibberish, imitating as closely as possible the tongues on the rest of the tape. The linguists spotted the deception immediately. "That's not language," one man said. "That's just noise." [7]

Wycliffe Bible translators have surveyed the languages of the world, and they estimate that there are still thousands of languages that have not yet been committed to writing and generally made known. Hence the fact that many gifts of tongues have not been recognized is not surprising. Many charismatics do not claim that each tongue is a bona fide language,

[7]John L. Sherrill, *They Speak With Other Tongues* (Lincoln, Va.: Chosen Books, Ltd., 1964), p. 101.

and in any case they would point to Paul's phrase, "If I speak in the tongues of men *and of angels*" (1 Cor. 13:1, italics mine). What are the tongues of angels? Could we understand them? Many advanced linguistic analyses have been made, but they are beyond the scope of a practical book of this nature.

There are two types of tongues. First, the gift of tongues that is used in a public meeting. Paul makes it clear that this is a gift that should never be practiced unless there is an interpreter present: "If any speak in a tongue, let there be only two or at most three, and each in turn; and let one interpret. But if there is no one to interpret, let each of them keep silence in church and speak to himself and God" (1 Cor. 14:27-28). Second, there is the gift of tongues to be used only in private devotions. This is basically a language for praise and adoration of our Lord. The prayer of adoration is often the most difficult, because we understand God so imperfectly, and also because no language devised by man can do justice to the person of God. This is where a gift of tongues can be of great blessing. The Christian, having reached the limits of his own language, can rise to the heights of adoration that once seemed impossible. He cannot understand the sounds or the words but is aware of the general feeling of worship. Paul makes a distinction between prayer with the mind and prayer with the spirit, "What am I to do? I will pray with the spirit and I will pray with the mind also; I will sing with the spirit and I will sing with the mind also" (1 Cor. 14:15).

Many Christians have found it possible to engage in this type of prayer not only in time set aside for devotions but, as Michael Green has pointed out, "Many people pray in tongues while driving a car or washing the dishes—their mind can be employed elsewhere."[8] There are many who declare that they have found a new freedom and uplift in their prayer life through this gift.

Paul states that "one who speaks in a tongue speaks not to

[8]Green, *I Believe in the Holy Spirit,* p. 164.

150

men but to God; for no one understands him, but he utters mysteries in the Spirit." And again, "He who speaks in a tongue edifies himself" (1 Cor. 14:2, 4). This is said in the context that prophecy is more important than tongues, but it in no way invalidates the gift of tongues. When Paul writes that speaking in a tongue edifies himself he is referring to the process of building oneself up. The word edifice is not much used today, but fifty years ago the phrase, "It is a fine edifice," simply applied to a building. The Bible is full of instructions to help us to grow as Christians.

John Stott has covered this ground fully but concludes, "Now in the light of this consistent New Testament emphasis on edification as a ministry to others, and to the Church; what are we to make of the one and only exception which says that the tonguespeaker 'edifies himself'? Surely there must be at least some degree of irony in what Paul writes, for the phrase is almost a contradiction in terms. Self-edification is simply not what edification is all about in the New Testament."[9]

This seems to be an extraordinary statement. John Stott has spent much of his life in encouraging other Christians to "edify themselves" by Bible study and other means. Many of us respect him highly for the discipline of his own devotional life that "edifies him" or "builds him up spiritually." We wonder why he should be so dubious about one of many aids that people find helpful.

Even though we recognize that tongues speaking is a way of edifying ourselves, it needs to be stressed that it is not the only one, or even the principal one. However much time is spent in exercising this gift it will not give us a knowledge and grasp of the Bible, which is so important.

Paul writes, "I will pray with the spirit and I will pray with the mind also" (1 Cor. 14:15). Paul is explaining that there is room for praying in an ordinary known language. He goes on to make the same point about singing. There is a place for orthodox singing of hymns and there is a place for "singing in the

[9]Stott, *Baptism and Fullness,* p. 115.

spirit." To be in a congregation where "singing in the spirit" takes place is a wonderful experience. The first time I heard it I was so unprepared that it was difficult to absorb what was happening and to understand it in a biblical perspective. However, I did try to analyze it and wrote a description while it was taking place. The singing had no human leader. It began quietly with a few people, and soon a large proportion of the congregation had joined in. There were no recognizable words, but an assortment of voices each adding its own distinctive contribution. Many complex melodies wove in and out, but there were no discords. It was a marvelously rich musical tapestry, gradually subsiding and then swelling out again with full richness. Then, almost suddenly, it came to an end and I realized that I was sorry it had finished. It had an ethereal beauty. I have observed it in large congregations and in small groups, but I have also been in congregations where one or two "tried to start it off," and it petered out and was very anticlimactic.

Many Christians have testified to the emotional therapy of tongues, as well as its spiritual help. This therapeutic value is stressed by Morton T. Kelsey, an Episcopalian minister and psychologist, who does not himself speak in tongues but has had much experience with those who do. Tongues have often been abused, but then they have also been of untold blessing to many.

Having dealt with the eight gifts listed in order of priority at the end of 1 Corinthians 12, we must turn next to the spiritual gifts mentioned earlier in the chapter.

UTTERANCE OF WISDOM AND UTTERANCE OF KNOWLEDGE

"To one is given through the Spirit the utterance of wisdom, and to another the utterance of knowledge according to the same Spirit" (1 Cor. 12:8-9). As Leon Morris points out, these two words are so similar that it is not easy to see exactly what Paul means. William Barclay suggests that *wisdom* means to know the deep things of God and that *knowledge* refers to the more practical type of knowledge, so important in the administration of church affairs. The wide difference of views expressed by charismatic writers makes it clear that dogmatism in the matter is dangerous.

Donald Gee refers to the fact that there is a difference of views but states that after many years of thought on the subject he is convinced that these gifts are concerned with preaching and teaching. First, the receiving of knowledge and understanding the things of God; second, the ability to impart knowledge to others. Although this view is not common among most charismatic and noncharismatic circles, I believe that Donald Gee is correct. Interestingly enough, the same view is taken by a recent Roman Catholic writer, Donald L. Gelpi, a charismatic.

The RSV rendering of the word "utterance" is certainly nearer to the original than is the King James rendering "word." Utterance would certainly be in accord with teaching and preaching. If it does refer to teaching and preaching it makes good sense. Paul writes, "Now we have received not the spirit of the world, but the Spirit which is from God, that we might understand the gifts bestowed on us by God. And we impart this in words not taught by human wisdom but taught by the Spirit, interpreting spiritual truths to those who possess the Spirit" (1 Cor. 2:12-13).

Few things are more thrilling (or more rare) than to listen to a God-equipped expositor open up the Word of God. There seems to be some men who, when they come to a complicated passage of Scripture, are able to drive straight to the heart of the matter, and make it sound deceptively simple.

There are certainly two different gifts involved in good exposition. First, there is the gift of understanding the passage of Scripture; this does not bypass the intellect, but makes good use of a well-stocked mind and an adequate library. But however clearly a man may understand Scripture, his understanding is of little use to the church unless it is accompanied by the gift of expression. The requirements, then, are that a man be gifted to understand the things of God and to put them clearly into words to communicate them to others. These things can and should be worked on, but we still depend upon spiritual equipping.

FAITH

"To another faith by the same Spirit" (1 Cor. 12:9). This is not to be confused with "saving faith," by which we come to know the Lord, but is a separate and distinct gift. I have asked for this gift but, as far as I can judge, I have never received it. However I have no doubt that it exists. John writes that "this is the confidence which we have in him, that if we ask anything according to his will he hears us" (1 John 5:14).

No man knows completely the recesses of his own being, but to the extent of my self-knowledge I am utterly convinced that there is absolutely nothing God cannot do. My problem is that often I do not know what is "according to his will." It seems to me that the "gift of faith" is intimately involved with knowing the will of God. When we think of this faculty the names of George Mueller and Hudson Taylor spring to mind. I believe that there are many unknown Christians who have this gift. From my experience I am inclined to believe that it is more often found among women than men. I would not be dogmatic about that but I have benefited greatly in my own ministry by such women who have shared my ministry by their prayers.

I would suggest that in our own day George Verwer of Operation Mobilization may be another who has this "gift of faith." He dares to take incredible steps of faith, because he apparently has an uncanny knowledge that such steps are in God's will. Others may blindly "believe" that a certain unusual step is right, but without their actions seeming to receive any confirmation from the Lord. It is not enough to convince one's self that an apparently illogical step is God's will; it must actually *be* God's will.

DISCERNING OF SPIRITS

"To another the ability to distinguish between spirits" (1 Cor. 12:10). The gift of discerning of spirits seems to be very rare, and yet it is more important in our day because of the great revival in the exercise of the gifts of the Spirit. We have already noted that almost every gift can be counterfeited by satanic or selfish power. To keep a charismatic meeting under real control, the "gift of discernment" is greatly needed, but it is often missing.

The church at Corinth greatly exaggerated the place of spiritual gifts, and the gift of discernment was therefore needed. I believe that we would be much nearer to revival if we had elders in charismatic circles who were able and willing to exercise discernment, and then to risk unpopularity by excercising discipline in the body of Christ. Excesses would be controlled and the members of the body would be built up.

An English Pentecostal writes in a very old book, "The gifts of the Spirit, apart from speaking in tongues for personal worship, should never be used in private or in the home. It is necessary for every word to be judged, and therefore the only safe place to prophesy is in the church, where it can be judged."[10]

John wrote, "Beloved, do not believe every spirit, but test the spirits to see whether they are of God; for many false prophets have gone out into the world" (1 John 4:1).

The gift of discernment is of necessity used by a mind that is critical as well as loving, and it is always possible that the critical aspect will overshadow the love. This gift calls for watchfulness and great humility.

Another list of spiritual gifts is found in Ephesians 4. It is much briefer, referring to only five gifts. Most of these are parallel to the list of gifts in 1 Corinthians 12 and also in the same order, but there are two important additions: "some evangelists, some pastors and teachers" (Eph. 4:11).

EVANGELISTS

There is a great deal of misunderstanding today about the nature of evangelism. When we hear the word "evangelist" we

[10]W. G. Hathaway, *Spiritual Gifts in the Church* (London: Elim Publishing Co., 1933), pp. 72-73.

155

tend to think of great auditoriums, massive publicity, and a man with a great personality. It is helpful to try to look at the subject in a biblical perspective. Actually, there is not a great deal of material about evangelism in the New Testament. It is only referred to twice apart from the reference, ". . . some evangelists . . ." (Eph. 4:11).

There is only one man who is called an evangelist in the Bible, and he is Philip. "On the morrow we departed and came to Caesarea; and we entered the house of Philip the evangelist" (Acts 21:8). His activities after Pentecost are mentioned in two places. In Acts 8 we read that he went to Samaria, "and proclaimed to them the Christ. And the multitudes with one accord gave heed to what was said by Philip, when they heard him and saw the signs which he did" (Acts 8:5-6). In this case he was filling a role much like that of an evangelist today. Later in the same chapter we see him talking to one man, the Ethiopian eunuch, and we read, "Then Philip opened his mouth, and beginning with this scripture he told him the good news of Jesus" (Acts 8:35).

The point that needs to be grasped is that Philip was as much an evangelist when talking to one person, as when he was talking to the multitudes. There are various definitions of an evangelist. I would define him as a person with the God-given ability to bring people to faith in Jesus Christ. We have all known of people who could present the good news of Christ, but who never seemed to be able to bring people to a decision.

Today I heard a preacher say that every Christian should be a "soul winner." I no more believe that everyone should be a soul winner than I believe that everyone should speak in tongues or be a preacher.

Having spent much of my life in student work I have met dozens of men and women who could not preach, but who had a wonderful gift of bringing people to faith in Christ. I have known others who asked me to pray with them that they might also receive the gift of evangelism. Sometimes God has granted the gift and at other times He has not. As with preaching, much can be done in terms of training; but then there is a real danger of having more faith in methods and formulas than in God Himself. It is impossible to overemphasize this today when every conceivable slick method of manipulating people is used in evangelism.

Recently, I talked to a young lady who complained that when she was introduced to a man, he ignored her greeting, but said, "Are you saved?" She was offended, and rightly so. Phillips translates 1 Corinthians 13:5 as follows, "Love has good manners." Although we are called to be "persuaders of men," that does not give liberty for bad manners or for high-pressure tactics that antagonize men rather than persuade them.

Paul was not described as an evangelist, although he was greatly used in evangelism. He used the word to Timothy, "do the work of an evanglist, fulfil your ministry" (2 Tim. 4:5).

It is right for a person to ask for the gift of leading people to faith in Christ, and we should all be trying to do the work of an evangelist. We must leave the matter of results with God. We are encouraged by the Scripture which says, "He who reaps receives wages, and gathers fruit for eternal life, so that sower and reaper may rejoice together. For here the saying holds true, 'One sows and another reaps.' I sent you to reap that for which you did not labor; others have labored, and you have entered into their labor" (John 4:36-38).

PASTORS AND TEACHERS

In most modern versions of the New Testament there is no comma between pastor and teacher in Ephesians 4:11. The two words were linked to describe one office in the local church: "some pastors and teachers."

We noted that there are three catalogs of gifts in the New Testament: one in 1 Corinthians 12, another in Ephesians 4, and one in Romans 12. It is essential to notice that only two gifts appear in all three lists. One is prophecy and the other is teaching.

"Pastor" is the Latin word for shepherd, and pastoring is a very honorable vocation. The word is applied to Jesus Himself: "I am the good shepherd. The good shepherd lays down his life for the sheep" (John 10:11).

One of the great benedictions of the Bible reads, "Now may the God of peace who brought again from the dead our Lord Jesus, the great *shepherd* of the sheep, by the blood of the eternal covenant, equip you with everything good that you may do his will, working in you that which is pleasing in his sight, through Jesus Christ; to whom be glory for ever and ever. Amen" (Heb. 13:20-21, italics mine). Here we see again that Jesus is called the Shepherd.

It is commonly believed in many circles that the most important and distinctive role of the pastor is visitation of the flock. Certainly that is part of it, but by no means the principal part. The fact that teaching occurs in all three lists of gifts, and that in Ephesians the man who possesses the gift is described as pastor and teacher makes it clear that the primary function of the pastor is to *teach*.

The passage in Ephesians 4 makes clear the purpose of the pastoral ministry: ". . . some pastors and teachers, to equip the saints, for the work of ministry, for building up the body of Christ, until we all attain to the unity of the faith and of the knowledge of the Son of God, to mature manhood, to the measure of the stature of the fulness of Christ; so that we may no longer be children, tossed to and fro and carried about with every wind of doctrine, by the cunning of men, by their craftiness in deceitful wiles. Rather, speaking the truth in love, we are to grow up in every way into him who is the head, into Christ" (vv. 11-15). If a man is not "apt to teach" he has no business being a pastor.

The passage makes it clear that pastoral teaching will produce Christian maturity and stability in the flock. It will also protect from "cunning men" and "every wind of doctrine."

I have dealt elsewhere with the importance of teaching, but I would add one more comment. When your church is looking for a pastor don't look for an administrator—look for a teacher.

Do not look for a crowd-pleaser—look for a teacher. Do not look for a good visitor—look for a teacher. If we get our priorities right much of the visitation and other work can and should be done by well-taught laymen who may be elders or deacons. The pastor is not called and paid to do all the work that the church members want to avoid; his main function is to *teach*. This is one of the few professions where the man called to be a leader is answerable to the people who pay his salary, who are supposed to be under his leadership. Paul was never in that position. When you have called a man to be your pastor, pray for him every day. He is the target of Satan, who will use criticism to destroy and break him if he can find men and women foolish enough to be his unwitting agents.

LIBERALITY

It is startling to find financial giving listed along with gifts such as prophecy and teaching. It is here for an important reason, "Having gifts . . . let us use them . . . he who contributes, in liberality" (Rom. 12:8). The word that Paul uses in this passage is *charismata*, and it refers to a God-given gift. Just as an evangelist has a gift bestowed by God, so a man who is entrusted with money must realize that this too is a gift from God and must be treated accordingly.

Paul writes that "it is required of stewards that they be found trustworthy" (1 Cor. 4:2). The New International Version translates this, "Now it is required that those who have been given a trust must prove faithful."

To possess the gift of evangelism or of teaching is a solemn responsibility; to possess financial means is just as solemn a responsibility. Just as a pastor or evangelist is expected to give of himself unstintingly, so must a man rich in material goods. The true test of his liberality will not be how much he gives, but how much he has left over after he has given.

In the New Testament financial giving is never regarded as something sordid or unspiritual, but as a sacred trust. A spiritual man will not use his giving to draw attention to himself. Jesus taught, "When you give alms, do not let your left hand know what your right hand is doing, so that your alms may be in secret; and your Father who sees in secret will reward you" (Matt. 6:3-4).

The church has not always been as wise over this matter as it should have been. I have known Christian work at home and overseas develop certain programs just because they were pet projects of people with money. Both those who give and those who dispose of gifts have at the same time a wonderful opportunity and a great responsibility in the Lord's service. "They shall not appear before the LORD empty-handed; every man shall give as he is able, according to the blessing of the LORD your God which he has given you" (Deut. 16:16-17). This theme runs throughout the Bible.

It is strange reasoning that allows a man to assume that there should be one standard of living for businessmen and a lower standard for pastors, etc. The Bible always speaks clearly about the duty of giving. Phillips' paraphrase of 2 Corinthians 9:1-6 reads, "Of course I know it is really quite superfluous for me to be writing to you about this matter of giving to fellow Christians, for I know how willing you are . . . For, it would never do if some of the Macedonians were to accompany me on my visit to you and find you unprepared! We (not to speak of you) should be acutely embarrassed, just because we had been so confident in you. This is my reason, then, for urging the brothers to visit you before I come myself, so that they can get your promised gift ready in time. For I should like it to be a spontaneous gift, and not money squeezed out of you. All I will say is that poor sowing means a poor harvest, and generous sowing means a generous harvest." These verses are forthright and in harmony with the teaching of the whole of Scripture. "One man gives freely, yet grows all the richer; another withholds what he should give, and only suffers want. A liberal man will be enriched, and one who waters will himself be watered" (Prov. 11:24-25).

After a lifetime in the ministry two things astonish me. One is the consistent generosity of some Christians and churches, and the other is the stinginess of others. It is not a coincidence that one of the first fruits of Pentecost was extreme generosity (Acts 2:45). The most generous giving I have seen is in the U.S.A. The most sacrificial has been in primitive cultures.

When Paul wrote, "Not that I seek the gift; but I seek the fruit which increases to your credit" (Phil. 4:17), he was referring to the principle that material stinginess leads to spiritual drought. "You will be enriched in every way for great generosity, which through us will produce thanksgiving to God; for the rendering of this service not only supplies the wants of the saints but also overflows in many thanksgivings to God.... Thanks be to God for his inexpressible gift" (2 Cor. 9:11, 12, 15).

FOR DISCUSSION

1. How many apostles do you believe there were?
2. Were apostles a gift to a local church or to the church universal?
3. Do you think that there are apostles today?
4. Is there some overlap between prophecy and teaching?
5. Is teaching and prophecy the same thing?
6. The prophet has two main functions. What are they?
7. In Old Testament prophecy did foretelling or forthtelling have the greater prominence?
8. Is teaching important? Why is it often neglected?
9. Does a "spirit-filled" teacher need to spend time in preparation?
10. Is exhortation a spiritual gift?
11. Which is the more important, teaching or healing?
12. Does God still perform miraculous healing today?
13. Do you think that there is healing in the Atonement?
14. How important is the ministry of helpers?
15. Give an illustration of the gift of helpers found in the Old Testament.
16. Is the gift of tongues an evidence of being filled with the Holy Spirit?
17. Why was the gift of tongues given to Cornelius?
18. Is typing as spiritual as preaching?

161

19. Do you think that speaking in tongues is intended to be used today? Give reasons.

20. What are the two different uses of the gift of tongues?

21. What is the main purpose of the private use of the gift of tongues?

22. Describe how the gift of faith may be different from saving faith.

23. Is the gift of discerning of spirits important?

24. Who in the New Testament is called an evangelist?

25. Is the gift of "pastor" linked with the gift of teaching?

26. There are three main lists of spiritual gifts listed in the New Testament. Which gifts appear in all three?

27. Is financial giving a material or a spiritual matter?

28. Does the Bible have much to say about financial giving?

16

Exorcism

Exorcism is not listed as a spiritual gift but we are living in a time when an extraordinary amount of witchcraft and demon possession are prevalent. It is not only practiced openly but is also made the subject of films. In response to this situation the church has often behaved sometimes with weakness, sometimes with what amounts to superstition; so some treatment of the subject seems to be called for. It will be helpful to divide the chapter into three parts.

THE DIAGNOSIS

One of the most difficult things to determine is whether the behavior patterns of a person are caused by some form of insanity, the use of drugs, or by demon possession. For many years in the small number of cases of demon possession that I have been called to deal with, I have asked one question. Do the symptoms appear to get worse or better in the presence of godly influence? I have known people who were unable to sit through a complete religious meeting, and the more spiritual authority there was in the meeting the sooner they had to leave. Similarly, the closer the individual seemed to come to the Lord through Bible reading and prayer, the worse their behavior seemed to be.

If the circumstances mentioned above did not fall into this category I would believe that the cause was not demon possession but rather a psychological disorder. If the person reacts against true spiritual power it is usually an evidence of demon possession. The diagnosis is not easy and the whole subject is one that I never involve myself in unless it is inevitable.

THE TREATMENT

I was once preparing a sermon on Revelation 12:11, "And they have conquered him by the blood of the Lamb and by the word of their testimony, for they loved not their lives even unto death." In preparation, the phrase that particularly drew my attention was, "by the word of their testimony." Most of my sources of information suggested that the phrase would apply to Christians who fearlessly gave testimony to their Christian faith. The phrase continued to puzzle me. I then tried to apply it to the confrontation between the Lord Jesus Christ and Satan in the wilderness. To whom did Jesus testify? To Satan of course. This suggested different channels for my thinking. Then I asked myself, How did Jesus testify to Satan? Again the answer was obvious: "It is written, It is written, It is written." So when confronting demonic powers I concluded that the testimony must be directed to Satan himself, and the testimony should be, "the sword of the Spirit, which is the word of God" (Eph. 6:17).

In this kind of situation the believer has authority. I also have made it a practice to address Satan verbally rather than in silent prayer; and to command him to come out and to quote several passages of Scripture including Revelation 12:11. I have deliberately not sought this type of confrontation because I believe it is a serious matter, and not to be embarked upon lightly. Nevertheless, I have seen glorious victories through this ministry.

SOME DANGERS AND ERRORS

There was an ugly experience that took place in England in 1975. The behavior of a certain man was strange and two pastors, one Methodist and the other Anglican (Episcopalian), concluded that it was a case of demon possession, and set out to exorcise the demons. They met with the man in a church, and in a session that lasted almost all night they reported afterward that they had cast out a large number of demons, and many of them they named. This involved great emotional strain, and having reached the place of exhaustion they let him go home; but they believed that there were still some demons they had failed to exorcise. The man returned to his home and almost immediately murdered his wife in a horrible and brutal manner. Needless to say, it was fully reported in all the national papers, and a committee of inquiry was set up in the Church of England for a full investigation. The ministers were obviously very sincere, and sought nothing for themselves. The whole incident was exploited by the media in a way that could only cause harm to the work of God.

I have known personally of cases where immature Christians tried exorcism only to find that it had a sad boomerang effect, and they themselves slipped visibly spiritually.

In 1975 the Rev. Trevor Dearing, and Anglican minister in England, gave up his pastorate to undertake an itinerant ministry of healing and exorcism; again it caused some interest in the media.

In the ministry of Paul the chief emphasis was always upon teaching, and exorcism was kept much in the background. There was no question of Paul or others making it their chief ministry, but it was simply a by-product that caused no drawn-out confrontation.

I am cautious indeed about some practices today. There seems to be a trend toward declaring the number of demons that possess a person and to name them: such as a spirit of lying, jealousy, impurity, and so on. I cannot find biblical evidence for such practice.

My daughter was in a church where the speaker asked for the windows to be closed lest the demons cast out returned in through them! It would be humorous if it were not so ridiculous. If Satan can make people believe that he does not exist he will be delighted; failing that, he will contrive to make

Christians more interested in himself than in Christ, and this will make him even more pleased.

Today when people have possibly been exposed to mind-changing drugs, or to psychiatric treatment, my advice would be to let well enough alone; or take action only if one or two mature and balanced Christians can be called on for advice and assistance.

FOR DISCUSSION

1. Why is the diagnosis of demon possession difficult?
2. Should we make the casting out of demons a central part of our ministry?
3. List some dangers of engaging in exorcism.
4. Did exorcism play a large part in the ministry of the apostle Paul?
5. Is exorcism listed as a spiritual gift?

17

The Holy Spirit and Divine Guidance

One of the many blessings of being a Christian is the knowledge that there is nothing haphazard or accidental in our lives. God has a plan and purpose for the life of every Christian, and He will not allow that plan to be frustrated by anything, or anyone. "We know that in everything God works for good with those who love him, who are called according to his purpose" (Rom. 8:28). Not that everything works together for *pleasure* but for *good*. We may not always understand the problems that invade our lives, but we can trust the One who controls them.

The Bible gives us clear guidance on matters of right or wrong in moral issues. We are living in a day when moral absolutes are not popular. Is premarital sex right or wrong? Many in the world would say that if there is a meaningful relationship it is permissible. The Bible is clear: "Do not be deceived; neither the immoral, nor idolaters, nor adulterers, nor homosexuals . . . will inherit the kingdom of God" (1 Cor. 6:9-10). Is it right for a Christian to marry a non-Christian? "Do not be mismated with unbelievers. For what partnership have righteousness and iniquity? Or what fellowship has light with darkness?" (2 Cor. 6:14).

However, there are many matters where the Bible does not give clear guidance. Should a person work for I.B.M. or General Electric? Should a person go to a seminary or not? Many people have taken an almost superstitious attitude toward divine guidance; and this is particularly so among the "newer charismatics." Donald Gee writes,

The Holy Spirit: Common Sense and the Bible

Since our theme is spiritual gifts in the work of the ministry it would take us a little off our line to deal with the grave problems raised by the habit of giving and receiving personal "messages" of guidance through the gifts of the Spirit. Yet this possesses an attraction that often can be described as little less than a fascination for many good people. Strangely enough, it seems to appeal to the cultured and educated almost more than to the unlearned and ignorant. I suppose we all desire to hear guiding words from the Lord. The Bible gives a place for such direction from the Holy Spirit, and we have the privilege of keeping a place for it also. It can provide some of the most precious Pentecostal experiences of a lifetime. But it must be kept in proportion. An examination of the Scriptures will show us that as a matter of fact the early Christians did *not* continually receive such voices from heaven. In most cases they made their decisions by the use of what we often call "sanctified commonsense" and lived quite normal lives. Many of our errors where spiritual gifts are concerned arise when we want the extraordinary and exceptional to be made the frequent and habitual.[1]

We must base our views on divine guidance from the Bible. One of the best known cases is that of Paul, "And they went through Phrygia and Galatia, having been forbidden by the Holy Spirit to speak the word in Asia. And when they had come opposite Mysia, they attempted to go into Bithynia, but the Spirit of Jesus did not allow them so, passing by Mysia, they went down to Troas. And a vision appeared to Paul in the night: a man of Macedonia was standing beseeching him and saying, 'Come over to Macedonia and help us.' And when he had seen the vision, immediately we sought to go on into Macedonia, concluding that God had called us to preach the gospel to them" (Acts 16:6-10). There is also an instance of guidance coming directly from God through the leaders of the church at Antioch, "While they were worshiping the Lord and fasting, the Holy Spirit said, 'Set apart for me Barnabas and Saul for the work to which I have called them.' Then after

[1]Gee, *Spiritual Gifts,* pp. 51-52.

168

fasting and praying they laid their hands on them and sent them off" (Acts 13:2-3).

A much more usual course of action is this one, "And after some days Paul said to Barnabas, 'Come, let us return and visit the brethren in every city where we proclaimed the word of the Lord, and see how they are' " (Acts 15:36).

God does not by-pass our intellect when we are called upon to make decisions. The Bible pattern seems to indicate that we should collect all the information we can, and then ask God to guide our judgment as to the correct decision. Of course it is useless to seek for God's guidance until or unless we are utterly committed to do His will whatever it may be, or whatever the cost. There will still be occasions when God may overrule our best judgment as He did with Paul and the call to Macedonia. That particular call was of tremendous importance to us for it led Paul to his first ministry in Europe with all the far-reaching blessings that flowed from that piece of obedience on the part of Paul. This type of guidance was the exception rather than the rule.

When I was a young Christian I had such an exaggerated view of guidance by the Holy Spirit that I almost asked Him to show me on which side of the street I should walk. Some of the great decisions of my life I still make out of an overwhelming conviction of the Spirit, rather than by a process of reasoning; but these are very much the exception rather than the rule.

For Discussion

1. Does the Bible give any guidance for living the Christian life?
2. Does the Bible insist upon moral absolutes in the lives of Christians?
3. What part should our intellect play in the making of decisions?
4. In the life of the apostle Paul were his decisions made on the basis of common sense or divine revelation?

18

The Strengths of the Charismatic Movement

When I arrived in North America in 1954 I soon recognized the fact that there was a great neglect of teaching on the person and work of the Holy Spirit. I came to the conclusion that one of the main emphases in my preaching ministry must be to try in a small way to rectify this deficiency. In 1978, it is difficult to realize that such a situation existed then because it has changed so dramatically in recent years.

Incidentally, although the subject was not adequately dealt with in Great Britain, we did have one advantage. Easter was a public holiday lasting from Good Friday to Easter Monday. It was unthinkable not to preach on the Resurrection at Easter. What was different about England was that Pentecost was also a public holiday, called Whitsun. Pastors were therefore expected to preach on Pentecost and the Holy Spirit on at least that one Sunday every year. This situation has now been changed by a government reorganization of public holidays.

The fact that the Holy Spirit is no longer the forgotten person of the Godhead is due almost completely to the influence of the charismatic movement; and for this we should be grateful. It is also true that thousands of people in solid evangelical churches find in this movement a spiritual freshness that before was unknown. Apart from the Christian Brethren there was little emphasis on the place of the layman in the work and ministry of the churches; and often professionalism reigned supreme. The openness of charismatic services, with time for free worship and ministry has gone a long way to correct this serious neglect.

The Strengths of the Charismatic Movement

Compared with services in many churches where worship often seems to be cold and impersonal, the sense of love and acceptance in charismatic churches is so warm that at its best it seems to engulf the visitor and church member alike. This is so different from other churches that at first it can be distasteful to the newcomer. In many, or even most such churches, a good handshake is not enough and hugging is the accepted form of greeting. I have rarely felt that this was contrived by man but rather was a genuine expression of Christian love.

When I first preached at a large and vigorous charismatic church I was distinctly uneasy. What would it be like? Would I feel embarrassed? In a word, I was very self-conscious. In the pastor's office before the service I sensed that the pastor was himself not without some quite understandable doubts about me! I came to the point directly: "I must explain that I have never preached in a charismatic church in the U.S.A. before, and I feel somewhat nervous." His face immediately lit up with a wide smile, and then he said frankly, "We haven't had anybody like you to preach before so I'm a bit nervous too. Let's pray about it." At once I felt accepted and at ease and my affection was immediate for this brother in Christ.

I walked into the pulpit with the pastor and his elders. I looked at the congregation. The building was not huge but there must have been double the number of people for which the building was planned. As we started to sing, many began to clap. Would they think me odd if I felt too self-conscious to join them? I looked again; I realized that no one was interested in me! Some clapped, some held both hands in the air, others held one hand up. Everyone was engrossed in what the service was to him and in his own communion with God. I experienced then a wonderful breaking down of artificial inhibitions; inhibitions that are so much part of our normal church life. This freedom is a real contribution that the charismatics have made to the church. At times it spills over to sloppiness, but an emphasis that breaks down stuffiness and makes people more open to the Lord and to each other is a valuable thing.

During the service I described, some of the "gifts" were in

operation. We had "tongues" with interpretation; praying for the sick; and "singing in tongues." It was all a wonderful uplifting experience. The service had been going well over an hour when I was called on to preach. I was mentally deciding what omissions I should make to my sermon to trim it down to fifteen minutes. Not a bit of it. The pastor in his humorous way told the congregation of our mutual encounter in his office. The congregation laughed, many clapped, and he said, "I have told brother Fife to take all the time he needs, and that we are used to sermons that last an hour." I enjoyed such freedom in preaching that I indeed did preach for almost an hour.

I had been accustomed to freedom in the student work I had been involved in for many years, but to find it to this extent in a downtown church on a Sunday morning was like a breath of fresh air.

I have known many Christians who have entered into a life of the "fullness of the Spirit" through this movement, who before had seemed confirmed in carnal attitudes. They had found a dimension that they had been looking for for years, and that had eluded them in ordinary church life. This is not to suggest that such a life of fullness began with the charismatic movement, or is at the present time confined to it. However, it would be true to say that thousands have been reached in this way who seemingly would have continued in the rut of suburban spiritual blight.

Another enormous contribution is that thousands, and probably millions, who knew nothing of regeneration, have found the living Christ; even as they often sought the "fullness of the Holy Spirit." My first awareness of this came in Latin America in the late 1950s. To find people by the hundreds who had become antichurch and antipriest because of years of exposure to dead forms and lifeless liturgy, and to find them stepping into the blinding healing light of the gospel was an experience not easily forgotten.

> Long my imprisoned spirit lay
> Fast bound in sin and nature's night;

172

The Strengths of the Charismatic Movement

Thine eyes diffused a quickening ray,
  I woke, the dungeon flamed with light;
My chains fell off, my heart was free;
  I rose, went forth, and followed Thee.

Charles Wesley

As one whose boyhood was lived in what would now be called a ghetto, I could not overlook the fact that these Pentecostals, and almost only they, were effectively reaching the really poor city dwellers around the world. This fact so impressed me that I wrote about it in the book which I co-authored, *Missions in Crisis,* which was published in 1961.

As Missionary Director of Inter-Varsity Christian Fellowship my work brought me into contact with some people who were active in the World Council of Churches. For some of them the gospel *was* the W.C.C. It was not difficult to see that enthusiasm for it was on the wane in the late 60s; apart of course from the committed ecumaniacs. In the light of this it was ironic, but wonderful, that with virtually no organization and no budget, the charismatic movement was smashing down denominational barriers all over the world. To see Mennonites, Roman Catholic nuns and priests, Presbyterians, Episcopalians, Methodists, Baptists, etc., all sharing together in great assemblies of love and worship was probably not quite as strange to us in interdenominational student work as it was to others. Nevertheless, it was certainly wonderful to see this, for what the W.C.C. had been unable to do with its extensive programs and large budgets, became true in the great wave of spiritual renewal.

Recently, I was in a very large charismatic church and the pastor asked for a show of hands, first of those who had come from a Methodist background, then those from a Baptist background, and lastly those from a Roman Catholic background. It was apparent that there was a similar number from all three.

Surely it was not by chance that John XXIII became Pope in 1958 and that the move to get Roman Catholics back to the Bible, and to open the church to new ideas, coincided with the great charismatic surge that probably affected Roman Catholics even more than Protestants. Whatever reservations we might retain on some issues, we dare not be unaware or ungrateful for the move of the Holy Spirit in renewal from Notre Dame to the Republic of Southern Ireland.

I have always found myself deeply moved by great gothic buildings, and even more by choral and organ music, and I love to listen to them for my own pleasure. I suspect that this response is more aesthetic than spiritual, and can be just as moving in a concert hall as in a cathedral. In humble buildings and through untrained lips, I believe the charismatic movement has provided an example of adoration and worship that is seldom equalled elsewhere. Its beauty and sincerity must surely set the courts of heaven ringing.

Another commendable trait of the charismatic movement is their attitude to giving. In Acts we learn that one of the first distinguishing marks of the young apostolic church was their attitude of generosity: "All the believers joined together and shared everything in common; they sold their possessions and goods and divided the proceeds among the fellowship according to individual need" (Acts 2:44-45, Phillips). I have observed that this characteristic is still found in charismatic churches, in Latin America, the United States, and Great Britain. The giving for foreign missions and to believers in great need is usually done sacrificially and cheerfully as taught in 2 Corinthians 9:7: "Let everyone give as his heart tells him, neither grudgingly nor under compulsion, for God loves the man who gives cheerfully. God can give you more than you can ever need, so that you may always have sufficient for yourselves and enough left over to give to every good cause" (Phillips).

FOR DISCUSSION

1. Is the place of laymen stressed in the charismatic movement?
2. What are some of the ways that people have been helped through the charismatic movement?

The Strengths of the Charismatic Movement

3. Has the charismatic movement been a means of evangelism?

4. Pentecostals have been very effective in reaching a section of society usually untouched. What is this section?

5. Has the charismatic movement helped to break down denominational barriers?

6. Has the charismatic movement contributed to the praise and adoration of God?

19

The Weaknesses of the Charismatic Movement

It is easy to point out shortcomings in any person or movement, but the test of the critic must be his motive. When I first saw the scope of a great movement of the Holy Spirit, I hoped and half-believed that it would mean an enormous revival that would affect all churches and denominations. That may yet come, but we are still far from it at the present time.

As I write about the weaknesses of the charismatic movement I write as one who for more than twenty years has tried to help bridge the gap between charismatics and non-charismatics. I am now tempted to think that the task is impossible. I address myself to the many friends I have in both mainline Pentecostal groups, and also the newer charismatic churches. I do so in the hope that imbalances may be corrected and the full potential of this great movement may be realized. There is danger in generalizations, and fortunately there are many exceptions to these comments of mine.

The greatest weakness that I detect in the movement is the lack of teaching. Donald Gee, who preached in Pentecostal circles for over forty years, was well aware of this danger, and dealt with it at some length in his book, *Spiritual Gifts in the Work of the Ministry Today.*

As we have noted elsewhere, the gift of teaching ranks high in the gifts of the Spirit. In commissioning His disciples, the Lord made it clear that they were commissioned to teach. Paul's life after his conversion was a life of teaching. Other things such as healing and exorcism were secondary and were by-products.

The Weaknesses of the Charismatic Movement

One consequence of this neglect of teaching is the failure to test new ideas against the Scriptures to make sure they are sound. In turn, this neglect has led, and is still leading, people into a variety of "fads." There is the fad of "discipling" or "shepherding" that has had unfortunate effects in Britain and South America, as well as in the United States.

Another fad is the "healing of the subconscious," which is a weird mixture of half truth and pseudo-psychology, and is used to probe into a person's distant past. One cannot imagine Paul engaging in such strange practices or being subjected to them. A somewhat similar fad is "the healing of the memory."

The charismatics are by no means the only ones who fail in this matter of teaching. There is a lack of scriptural exposition throughout the church of Christ which I find alarming.

I have written that one of the great contributions of the charismatics is that of praise and worship, but often this degenerates into the almost endless singing of choruses, interspersed with testimonies that are sometimes puerile. And even after a two-hour service the people leave without having had any real Bible teaching. Thank God for the fine exceptions when one gets both worship and good teaching, but they are greatly in the minority.

Another disappointment is the emphasis on *experience*. In fact, what people believe is usually colored far more by the experience of others than by teaching. Emphasis is placed more upon "feeling good" than upon having learned some Bible truth. Human experiences must always be measured by the Scripture, and if there is not a biblical authority it must be rejected. Testimonies have their place but it should be a small one.

Closely associated with this emphasis on experience and testimony is the emphasis placed on personality. If testimonies are overemphasized it is almost inevitable that people with an interesting experience are much in demand. Their aim is usually to help others and bring glory to God, but at times it becomes almost a cult of "personality." One example of this is Dennis Bennet. His experience as an Episcopalian minister who received the "gift of tongues" in 1960 is certainly interesting. However, it is pathetic that eighteen years later he is still traveling the world telling of this experience.

Related to this is the experience of some well-known people in show business, sport, or other public prominence. They become baptized and filled with the Spirit, and are then regarded as instant experts on every phase of the Christian life. The advice of Paul to Timothy is extremely important. Writing of the office of bishop or elder he says, "He must not be a recent convert, or he may be puffed up with conceit and fall into the condemnation of the devil" (1 Tim. 3:6).

It is ironic, but probably inevitable, that one of the great blessings of the movement should have caused one of its problems. Many pastors who were unregenerate have been brought to life in Christ. With little or no opportunity to mature they have had to exercise public responsibilities while at the same time trying to adjust to their own new experience as "babes in Christ."

It is perhaps less excusable when a "show business" personality is exploited. I once watched a charismatic program on T.V. Telephone lines were available so people could "phone in" questions, which were then answered live on the telecast. At the beginning of the program a film actress gave a testimony and explained that she had accepted Christ only thirty minutes before. She described what a wonderful experience it was. People were then encouraged to "phone in" their questions. She was fairly well-known, so soon the phones were busy. I was flabbergasted as this young lady, who knew virtually nothing about the Bible or the things of God, tried to answer a variety of complex questions that she was unqualified to answer. In contrast to this, when the British pop star Clif Richard became a Christian, he was wisely advised to keep a low profile until he had time to mature. He still has his regular show on the British Broadcasting Corporation. In 1976 he was selected to be the first pop star to hold a series of concerts in Soviet Russia. It was good that he had the intelligence and humility to "grow up" spiritually before becoming too vocal publicly on spiritual matters.

The charge has been made that great divisions have been caused by the charismatics. This is unfortunately true, but the faults have not all been one-sided. It is not surprising that in the first flush of enthusiasm they have said and done things that antagonized others. However, churches have sometimes been to blame in being too unloving and unwilling to be supportive and flexible. Even pastors who have great sympathy for the charismatics have found it almost impossible to integrate them into the life of the church.

Recently I was the pastor of a church in England, and just four miles away was a sister church that had "gone charismatic." A few of my members were bitter about the whole thing; most of them were a little suspicious but were basically tolerant. The other pastor and myself had some slight differences of view, but he was a godly man and had a loving spirit. Our personal relationship was excellent. It would have been natural and good for the two churches to have had united services occasionally, but it was impossible because of the attitudes on both sides. If we had planned a united service, some from the other church would have raised their hands in worship, and clapped during some of the singing. I knew only too well that some of my people would have been upset, and wrongly so.

We had reached the ridiculous position where I dare not raise my hands because of the attitude of my people, and the other pastor could not desist from raising his because of offending his congregation. Both of us were placed in a false position.

Perhaps it should be stated that tension and division are not inevitable. I knew a young lady who spoke in tongues every day in her private devotions, and the young lady who shared her apartment for two years did not even know that she was charismatic. On the other hand I have met many who not merely practiced the "gift of tongues," but also insisted upon propagating it. Leaders of Mission Boards have nearly all faced this problem. In such groups there has to be a willingness to be flexible on some issues. For example, to be a member of a truly interdenominational group you have to be flexible on subjects that are important but not fundamental, such as baptism. The same is true of the gift of tongues.

In charismatic groups there has been a tendency to accentuate the minor points and neglect the major ones. I think that this is often more true of the new charismatic groups than of the mainline Pentecostals. These things are not a novelty to them for they have lived with them for many years. Even so many missionaries accuse the Pentecostals of poaching or sheep stealing.

Another feature that has caused concern to many is the apparent neglect of theology. I have stated that the ecumenical nature of the charismatic movement is wonderful, and so it is. But what can we make of people who say, and write, that since receiving the "baptism and the fullness of the Spirit," they find that they have a greater love for the Mass and the Virgin Mary! Surely there should be more discernment and discrimination (in the best use of that word) on these and other matters. It seems that generally speaking, providing a person has had a similar experience to theirs, the charismatics are prepared to accept almost anyone, whatever doctrine they believe. This comes dangerously close to an existential outlook.

I have already dealt with a number of spiritual gifts, but in a general way it should be repeated that the tendency to devote more attention to tongues, healing, and exorcism than to teaching is utterly contrary to biblical example and precept. To quote Donald Gee once more:

> While the habit of using the gifts of tongues and interpretation of tongues for prophetical messages remains among us there are certain wise rules to be observed. A speaker in tongues should not normally interrupt an anointed preacher of the Word. The habit of immediately following an anointed sermon with utterance in tongues also is not to be recommended, for it only tends to distract from the impression already made by the Word. Usually these things arise from a Spirit-filled, but undis-

ciplined, believer's feeling a personal agreement with the Word preached. His own spirit is stirred within him and he mistakenly feels that it is the Spirit of God. Should this utterance be genuinely interpreted it usually turns out to be nothing exceptional, and only what the preacher would have said, or has already said, in any case. The whole habit is rooted in the mistaken idea that the utterance in tongues possesses a quality of supernatural inspiration not present in the ministry of the Word, and that idea arises from failure to recognize the better gifts of the same Spirit being manifested in preaching and teaching.[1]

Similarly the stress on supernatural guidance that by-passes the mind makes for great instability. Another strange tendency is that of meetings that are unnecessarily lengthy. I dislike the fact that many normal churches are ruled by the clock, but I have been to far too many meetings that go on and on, not because anything special is taking place but because the leaders seem to think that there is something spiritual about the sheer length of a meeting; as if blessing can be measured by the hour.

One matter I want to mention is that of the music and hymnody of the charismatics. When I was a teenager I sang gospel choruses with great gusto. When Scripture choruses began to gain in popularity I found that many of them were songs of real worship. I enjoyed them and used them in services in *addition* to hymns in regular hymn books. In a number of places where I have worshiped recently hymn books were not used at all, and in one church they did not even possess any. The standard of words and music of charismatics seem to have deteriorated in the last five years or so. It would be tragic if a whole generation of Christians grew up totally unaware of the enormous heritage of hymnody that we have inherited.

In recent years it has become popular in some charismatic circles to display the sign of a "dove" on automobiles, churches, and homes. I have already pointed out that a dove is

---

[1]Gee, *Spiritual Gifts,* p. 56.

a scriptural symbol of the Holy Spirit. When I see such symbols used it makes me feel that the biblical priorities have been reversed. I am reminded of what our Lord said of the Holy Spirit, *"He will glorify me*, for he will take what is mine and declare it to you" (John 16:14, italics mine). When I see such stress on the person of the Holy Spirit I believe the biblical priorities have been reversed.

For Discussion

1. Name one great weakness of the charismatic movement.
2. Are the charismatics the only ones who fail in the matter of teaching?
3. What place does experience have in the charismatic movement?
4. Name some difficulties that face ordained ministers who become regenerate through a charismatic experience.
5. Is there much emphasis on theology in the charismatic movement?
6. Do charismatic Christians sometimes get their priorities wrong?

20

A Sketch of the Charismatic Movement

To attempt a brief sketch of the history of the charismatic movement is to enter a minefield of difficulties. The biggest single problem is to define the word "charismatic." The word is derived from the Greek word *charisma* meaning "grace gifts" or spiritual gifts. We have seen that there are approximately twenty such gifts mentioned in the New Testament, and many of these, such as pastor/teacher, evangelist, helper, etc. have been in constant use throughout the long history of the church.

The general use of the word charismatic in our day has made its meaning much narrower. It is used almost exclusively to describe people who emphasize or practice the gift of tongues, and the gift of prophecy in the sense of forecasting future events.

Leaving aside for a moment these controversial gifts it must be obvious that many great heroes of church history have possessed and used a number of spiritual gifts. One thinks almost automatically of such people as John Wycliffe, Martin Luther, John Calvin, George Whitefield, Dwight L. Moody, Charles H. Spurgeon, Billy Graham, and others. In John Wesley's case it would seem that with his remarkable power in evangelism, teaching, and church planting he performed the work of an apostle. As we sketch the history of tongues speaking, it is essential that we recognize the fact that all those mentioned above were charismatic in the sense that they possessed a variety of the gifts of the Spirit. Though I use the term charismatic I do so with great reluctance because it is inadequate in definition.

There is another problem involved in attempting to write any history, however brief, and that is the matter of sources. Many who have written concerning the gift of tongues are so anxious to provide historical authority for it that they have treated as confirmed fact occurrences which are supported by only slender or doubtful evidence. The reverse is also true. Some are so prejudiced against tongues that they suppress evidence in its favor. The Welsh Revival is a useful illustration. To read some accounts of it is to be convinced that it was a thoroughly charismatic experience. Others describe the same revival and do not mention the gift of tongues at all.

At the end of the second century Irenaeus made a clear statement that both tongues and prophecy were in use in his day. Tertullian, the great North African apologist for the early church, also made clear references to tongues and prophecy in approximately A.D. 225. This seems clear evidence that the gift did not pass away when the apostles died. By the time of Augustine, at the end of the fourth century, the gift of tongues does seem to have passed away.

Morton T. Kelsey has dealt with the history of tongues in some detail in his book *Speaking With Tongues* (Epworth Press). He writes that the gift of tongues has always been present in the Greek Orthodox Church and that the Patriarch of Constantinople stated that his church had always recognized and controlled the gift of tongues (p. 43). I have inquired about this of local Greek Orthodox clergy but could obtain neither confirmation nor denial.

Souer in his *History of the Christian Church* states that Martin Luther was a "speaker in tongues," but I do not know what his authority is for this statement. Most other authors make no such claim.

Some claim that John Wesley spoke in tongues, but though he seems to have been aware of the gift of tongues, the evidence that he used it is extremely slender. A far more likely person seems to be one of Wesley's preachers, Thomas Walsh. He wrote in his diary on March 8, 1750, "This morning the Lord gave me a language I knew not of, raising my soul to Him in a wondrous manner."[1]

Jonathan Edwards was born in the same year as John Wesley, 1703. This man, whom Perry Miller describes as the greatest philosopher/theologian produced by North America, was greatly used by God. He saw great revivals in his church in Northampton, Massachusetts in 1734-35, and in 1740-41. He was used by God in the Great Awakening. One of the characteristics of his ministry was that individuals were so overcome by a conviction of sin that they cast themselves prostrate on the floor, groaning with guilt. This was not peculiar to the Great Awakening for it was also characteristic of revivals in other countries in later days. This raises the question of whether the phenomenon is similar to what today's charismatics call being "slain in the Spirit." Since few of these happenings have been described minutely and accurately there must remain a question mark. One thing that should be noted is the great difference between conversion experiences of a century or more ago and those of today. In past centuries many men were bowed down by a conviction of guilt and sin that lasted for weeks until the sunshine of Christ broke through and brought them the joy of forgiveness of sin and fellowship with Christ.

Many of these men were born and raised in a cultural atmosphere which acknowledged the greatness of God; indeed, many revivals were harvests reaped from soil prepared by Calvinist preaching. How different is the situation today, when the personality of the evangelist often seems to overshadow the person and glory of Christ.

THE CUMBERLAND PRESBYTERIAN CHURCH

The history of this church is older and much more interesting than most people seem to realize. Its origins are among the

[1]Michael Harper, *As At the Beginning* (London: Hodder & Stoughton), p. 21.

Scotch-Irish pioneers who had settled in Kentucky and Tennessee. It has been said of those hardy settlers that "they kept the Sabbath and anything else they could lay their hands on."

Many of these settlers were Presbyterians, and after days of prayer and fasting signs of revival were evident in 1796-97. In 1799 this revival spread and there were many cases of prostration under the Spirit. These were frontier days and clashes with Indians were common. The most outstanding geographic feature of this locality was and is the Cumberland Gap, a pass through the Cumberland Mountains at the joint boundary of Virginia, Kentucky, and Tennessee.

The first camp meeting was held in Red River, Logan County, Kentucky. There are differences of opinion as to whether it was in 1799 or 1800. The original camp meeting consisted of whole families traveling in wagons to some central spot. While the families lived in their wagons for a week or more, meetings would be held at which great blessing was experienced. These camp meetings were later to become common among the Methodists and Baptists.

Out of the womb of this great Second Awakening was born the Cumberland Presbyterian Church. It is basically Presbyterian in its church government but is Arminian in its doctrine. Geographically, it kept pace with the ever-advancing frontier.

The authoritative historical work on this subject is the *History of the Cumberland Presbyterian Church* by McDonnold, published in 1888. This small denomination dates its history back to 1800 and published its first Confession in 1814, half a century before the Civil War.

In McDonnold's history there is a great emphasis on spiritual power, Paraclete baptism, miraculous healing, prostrations, and so on. There is no reference to tongues speaking, but Rev. Larry Moss, who is very active in the charismatic circles of the Cumberland Presbyterian Church and to whom I owe this information and literature, believes strongly that references to tongues were edited out of the book because it was an unwelcome subject when the book was written in 1888.

A Sketch of the Charismatic Movement

There are reports of several incidents of tongues speaking in the USA from 1875 on, most of them in the nineteenth century. There are a few incidents recorded in the Midwest as early as 1875.

In 1887 the Christian and Missionary Alliance was founded by Dr. A. B. Simpson. It has become a large denomination with a magnificent missionary program. In its early years it was relatively tolerant of those who had the gift of tongues. Its attitude is best summed up by a dictum of Dr. Simpson's in 1907. "Seek not, forbid not." This basic attitude was reaffirmed approximately sixty years later.

The early part of this century saw a great international quickening of pace. One great outbreak occurred in Topeka, Kansas, in 1900 and was followed by others, including those in Texas in 1905 and in Oslo, Norway, and Sunderland, England, in 1907. The following years saw such movements in Norway, Germany, Switzerland, and Australia.

AZUSA STREET

So much has been written about the Pentecostal revival which took place in a remodeled stable in Azusa Street, Los Angeles, in 1906 that we need do little to expand upon it. However, some details of it must be mentioned because it became such a watershed for the charismatic movement.

The revival began when a black evangelist was invited to preach at a series of meetings in April, 1906. At first this Pentecostal movement was confined to blacks, but they were soon joined by Caucasians. People came from all over the country to attend these meetings, which continued for several years. The fullest account of this movement is given by Klaude Kendrick in *The Promise Fulfilled* (Gospel Publishing House). Morton Kelsey claims that twenty-six denominations trace their beginnings to the events at Azusa Street, including the Assemblies of God and the Foursquare Church.

From this time and place the advance of tongues speaking

was rapid and spread throughout the world. Generally speaking the mainline denominations treated all this with suspicion—which suspicion was returned by the Pentecostal groups.

Immediately after World War II the National Association of Evangelicals was formed, and this did much to bring together missionary leaders of the Assemblies of God with non-Pentecostal leaders of dozens, or perhaps even hundreds of other missionary societies. As has often happened, it was developments on the mission field that led to events at home and that did most to break down walls of mutual suspicion. Certainly Dr. Henry Van Dusen, when president of Union Theological Seminary New York in the 1950s, was most impressed by what he saw of the Pentecostal missionary work in Latin America. I mentioned this fact when I lectured at Yale Divinity School in March 1958.

In 1957 Rev. Paul Morris, a Presbyterian minister in Jamaica, New York, received the gift of tongues. In the late 1950s I was sufficiently impressed by these reports to ask Rev. Melvin Hodges to arrange for me to see something of the work of the Assemblies of God in Latin America, and he arranged for me to visit El Salvador. I was very impressed by what I saw, so much so that I wrote of it at some length in a book I co-authored with Dr. Arthur Glasser. This book was published in 1961 and entitled *Missions in Crisis*.

At this time I was on the staff of the InterVarsity Christian Fellowship, and in the fall of 1962 we received reports of an outbreak of tongues-speaking in the IVCF chapter at Yale. This was examined on the spot by Dr. Charles Hummel, at that time our field director.[1] On his return to headquarters he reported his findings to Mr. Charles Troutman, our General Director. The senior men in IVCF discussed the incident and saw its implications. We were aware of the fact that various stu-

---

[1]This has been treated thoroughly by Charles Hummel in a book entitled *Fire in the Fireplace,* published by IV Press.

dents, and at least one staff member, had received the gift of tongues. I was asked to write a statement outlining the position of the movement on tongues-speaking. It must be remembered that IVCF is a movement that works with all denominations, and therefore some members favor one form of baptism while others practice another. We can agree on the basics and not propagate these minor disputable questions.

In the statement I wrote I explained this and declared that any staff member had freedom to practice the gift privately and to answer questions about it, but that if he felt he had to propagate it he should seek a ministry outside the ranks of IVCF. My statement was accepted with minor amendments and to the best of my knowledge it is still the policy of the movement.

The Lutheran Story

According to Larry Christenson, in the summer and fall of 1961 small groups of Lutherans in widely scattered areas of the United States began to have a charismatic experience. He reports that in 1963 the charismatic renewal spread to Lutherans in Germany, Scandinavia, Eastern Europe, Africa, Asia, Australia, and South America. He goes on to report that in the decade that followed 1961 at least 10 percent of the Lutherans in the U.S.A. either had received the blessing or were favorable to it (*The Charismatic Renewal Among Lutherans,* Lutheran Charismatic Renewal Service). In a denomination that numbers some 2,492,355 baptized members, that proportion certainly makes a large number. Other Lutherans have claimed that the figure of 10 percent is too high and should be about 5 percent. Exact figures are impossible to obtain but obviously the number is significant.

What has been the effect of this movement in the Lutheran Church? It varies in the different Lutheran Synods. Although no statistics are available, some Lutherans I have spoken to hold the opinion that there have been a greater number of people and pastors who have had a charismatic experience in the Missouri Synod than in any other. The Missouri Synod is more conservative in its theology than other Lutheran bodies, and it is also less flexible. Generally they have taken a firm stand against the charismatics and one Lutheran pastor suggested to me that may be the reason they have more crises than other Lutheran groups.

Generally the gifts of tongues and prophecy are not in evidence in the main worship services but are confined to home prayer and study groups. Even in these groups the gifts are exercised in a quiet and restrained way. One Lutheran acquaintance of mine told me that he did not regard the Full Gospel Businessmen's Fellowship as charismatic. I expressed astonishment, and he explained that he thought the FGBMFI were too unrestrained, and should be called Pentecostal.

Larry Christenson records that the Lutheran Charismatic Renewal Services was started at the suggestion of Catholic charismatics who felt that without it the charismatics in the Lutheran churches would drift away to Pentecostal churches.

Lutheran ministers I have spoken to share Larry Christenson's belief in baptismal regeneration. Christenson goes so far as to say that rebaptism is impossible (p. 66). In contrast, I have learned by talking to lay Lutherans that in practice most are rebaptized after they have experienced renewal.

Pastor Norris L. Wogen states in *The Shadow of His Hand* that there is little opposition to the charismatic renewal in the Lutheran church today.[2] It may be that others of us have much to learn from our Lutheran brothers, but he also states that it is good that men with liberal theological views and those with conservative views can have great fellowship in the renewal.

I cannot personally accept that liberal theology is a matter to be overlooked. I do, however, respect these men and what they are doing to bring life to the spiritually dead.

---

[2]Norris L. Wogen, *The Shadow of His Hand* (Minneapolis: Bethany Fellowship, Inc., 1975), p. 116.

A Sketch of the Charismatic Movement

THE ROMAN CATHOLICS

Some extraordinary developments have taken place within the Roman Catholic Church since Pope John and Vatican II, but surely the most unexpected development has been the Catholic charismatic renewal. It began with four people at Duquesne University in Pittsburgh in 1967. By June 3, 1973, 25,000 people, 600 priests, eight bishops, and Cardinal Suenens held a mass at Notre Dame to celebrate the Catholic charismatic renewal. The 1977 directory records that there are 3,000 Catholic charismatic prayer groups in the USA and Canada.

By any standards this growth in nine years is almost unprecedented. It is understandable that charismatics regard the renewal as an answer to Pope John's prayer at Vatican Council II: "Renew Thy wonders in this our day, as by a new Pentecost." Informal estimates give the figure of fifteen million charismatic Catholics in the USA in 1977, but of course no accurate statistics are available.

The chief concentration of these groups is in the Midwest, but groups are scattered throughout the world. Naturally there are variations from place to place and even from parish to parish. Although priests are sometimes involved, the charismatic renewal is led to a large extent by nuns and lay people. I have been informed of this in connection with the Republic of Southern Ireland as well as with the United States.

I have attended a Roman Catholic charismatic mass, and although a prior commitment compelled me to leave after about two hours, the experience made an indelible impression. There were a number of nuns present, some dressed in habits and many in ordinary street clothes. There were also a few priests, but up to the time I left the meeting the proceedings were completely in the hands of laymen. The atmosphere was one of joy, love, and exuberance. A great deal of emotion was displayed, and there were several periods of singing in tongues.

191

The experience of these various groups emphasizes the amazingly ecumenical nature of the whole charismatic movement.

THE ARMENIAN STORY

The Armenian story covers almost 100 years and is the most remarkable of all the aspects of the charismatic awakening. It will be important to outline a little of the rich Armenian history. Armenia lies between the Black Sea and the Caspian Sea, partly in Turkey and partly in Soviet Russia. Today there are few Armenians left in Turkey but many in Russian Armenia, including distinguished scientists.

As a race, the Armenians date back to the seventh century B.C., the time of the Persian Empire. The whole area is dominated by Mount Ararat, with its altitude of 17,000 feet. On the plateaus grows grass rich in protein; this area has produced great horses and superb cavalry.

The history of the Armenians is rich and varied but also very sad; as a buffer state they have suffered repeatedly at the hands of their powerful neighbors. For example, the Turkish massacres of 1895 and 1914-1918 shocked the world.

I am indebted to three Armenians for the following facts, some of which have never before appeared in print. One source is Dr. Kenell Touryan, the second his father, Pastor Vahram Touryan, and the third, Mr. Demos Shakarian.

Dr. Ken Touryan is in a unique position to provide information. He came to the USA in 1956, having completed his undergraduate studies at the American University in Beirut. He received a master's degree at the University of Southern California, then attended Princeton University to gain another master's degree and a Ph.D. He now holds a responsible position at the Sandia Laboratories in Albuquerque, New Mexico. He also speaks six languages, including English, Arabic, Armenian, and Russian. His scientific qualifications and array of languages have opened to him many doors for ministry, especially among scientists and Armenians. The capital of Soviet

A Sketch of the Charismatic Movement

Armenia is Erevan, one of the oldest continuously inhabited cities in the world. It has been occupied since 2750 B.C. Dr. Kenell Touryan has visited Soviet Armenia and was exceptionally well-treated, first because of his scientific credentials and second because of his fluency in the Armenian language.

Mr. Demos Shakarian is the founder of the Full Gospel Businessmen's Fellowship International and author of *The Happiest People on Earth* (Fleming H. Revell).

Pastor Touryan and Demos Shakarian's father both lived in Turkey at the base of Mount Ararat. The Shakarian family, together with other Pentecostals, emigrated to Los Angeles just after 1900 in response to the repeated warnings of Efim, "the little prophet." They thereby escaped the frightful massacres begun by the Turks on April 24, 1914. The Little Prophet emigrated with them to Los Angeles where he died in 1915. As a sidelight on this history, Adolf Hitler knew of these massacres, and during his persecution of the Jews in World War II he said that the world had not gone to war to rescue the Armenians, and would not do so to protect the Jews.

Pastor Touryan was a member of a family of nine who belonged to the Orthodox Armenian Church. In the massacres his father was shot, a sister committed suicide to avoid being raped, and with only two exceptions the rest of the family died of starvation or were clubbed to death. Pastor Touryan's life was saved by a Turkish sheikh, and he was brought up as a Muslim. The marvelous story of his conversion and ministry is too long for this book, but he emigrated to the USA in 1956, and has been pastor of two Armenian churches in Pasadena and Los Angeles for more than twenty years.

In August, 1977, Dr. Kenell Touryan was the speaker at an Armenian youth conference in Southern California. Present at the conference was a young man who had recently emigrated from Soviet Armenia. In a small prayer meeting he prayed in fluent Armenian and then switched into another language, which others present assumed was Russian. Dr. Touryan took him aside afterward and said, "That wasn't Russian you were praying in, was it?" The young man admitted that it was not, but that he had been praying in tongues. He told Dr. Touryan that a great charismatic revival was taking place in Soviet Armenia. In December, 1977, I related these facts to Dr. Arthur Glasser, Dean of the Fuller Theological Seminary School of World Mission. Dr. Glasser replied that this seemed to confirm reports he had received of a great people's movement taking place in southern Russia. This charismatic revival is said to affect between ten and twenty thousand people there.

There is yet another incident in the saga of the Armenians. Mr. Demos Shakarian reported to me that in October, 1977, he was speaking at a charismatic meeting in the town of Vernon, in British Columbia, Canada. During his talk he mentioned that in the last century Russian Pentecostals had been banished to Siberia, and that from there some had made their way to China and others to Finland. He noticed a stir in the congregation, and was told that forty of those present were grandchildren of those who had settled in China. He spoke to them after the meeting and found that the Chinese Pentecostals of Russian descent had received a prophecy in the 1940s warning them that persecution was coming and that they should leave China. Many made their way first to Australia and then to British Columbia, and there are approximately 300 now living in the town of Vernon.

To revert to the writings of Efim, "the Little Prophet," Demos Shakarian reports that he saw the original papers, written a century ago and brought to Los Angeles by Efim at the turn of the century. Dr. Touryan, his father, and I have been trying to trace these papers for four months. It is the custom of the Armenians to hand such items down from father to son, but at the time of writing this book we have been unable to trace the whereabouts of these papers. This neither proves nor disproves their validity, but there is no disputing the fact that a fairly large group of Armenian Pentecostals did emigrate from Turkey to Southern California, and that in so doing they and their relatives escaped the Armenian Massacres of 1914-1918.

A Sketch of the Charismatic Movement

THE ASSEMBLIES OF GOD

The work of the Assemblies of God is a direct result of the meetings at Azusa Street in 1906. An organized body was formed in April, 1914, when the Assemblies of God formally adopted a constitution in Hot Springs, Arkansas, and in an Act of that year they were officially incorporated. Coincidentally, April, 1914, also saw the beginning of the massacre of the Armenians by the Turks.

The spread of the Assemblies has been rapid and unusually well-documented. Details of doctrine, church government, and expansion have been well set out by Klaude Kendrick in his book *The Promise Fulfilled*. A feature in *U.S. News and World Report* in April, 1977, stated that the Assemblies of God led all denominations over a ten-year period, with a growth in membership of 37 percent. Statistics in the General Secretary's report for 1977 indicate that the world-wide adherents number approximately six million.

Dr. Melvin L. Hodges, Associate Professor of Coordination of Missions Science at the Assemblies of God Graduate School, has kindly made available the following statistics: as of December 31, 1977 the Assemblies of God served 98 mission fields, employed 1,136 missionaries and 27,229 national ministers, and operated 167 Bible schools.

This short sketch can in no way do justice to the millions of charismatic Christians of all affiliations throughout the world. It must surely indicate, however, that the modern charismatic renewal is the greatest development in the church of Christ since the Reformation.

FOR DISCUSSION

1. Have some spiritual gifts been in operation throughout the history of the church?

2. Who was the great Christian theologian who referred to tongues and prophecy in A.D. 225?

3. What is a difference between many spiritual conversions in past centuries and most that take place today?

4. Where did the Cumberland Presbyterian church begin?

5. What attitude to tongues was taken by the Christian and Missionary Alliance?

6. What year and event did much to advance the charismatic movement in this century?

7. What percentages of Lutherans are reported as being charismatic?

8. Do you think that it is good that people of liberal and conservative theology minister together without theological issues being raised?

9. Give some details of how the charismatic movement has affected the Roman Catholic Church.

10. Where is Armenia geographically?

11. What did Adolf Hitler know about the Armenians?

12. There are reports that a great charismatic revival is taking place at the present time. Can you name the place?

21

Conclusion

An apochryphal story is told by Peter E. Gillquist that is worth repeating:

> It's late in the second year of Jesus' public ministry, and He is teaching a group of His followers on a Judean hillside. Among those in the crowd are two men who have not met before and who happen to be seated next to each other.
>
> While the Lord is revealing the things of God to the throng, the one man nudges the other and remarks, "Isn't He wonderful?"
>
> "He certainly is," whispers the second. "He healed me of blindness, you know."
>
> "He did!" says the first with surprise. "He healed *me* of blindness, too!"
>
> "That's amazing," the second man remarks, motioning to his new friend to pull away from the crowd a bit so their talking will not cause disturbance. "How did it happen?"
>
> "Well, this friend of mine—who was also blind—and I were sitting by the edge of the road just outside of Jericho. We could tell from the voices of an approaching crowd that the Lord was coming our way and would soon pass us on the road.
>
> "When He was within earshot, we yelled up to Him something like, 'Oh Lord, Son of David, give us your mercy.'
>
> "Jesus called over to us and said, 'What do you want Me to do for you?'
>
> "We said, 'Lord, we just want to be able to see.' And in a flash, we both had our eyesight restored."
>
> "Wait a minute!" says the second man, with a note of contempt in his voice. "There's no way it could have happened like that."

"What are you talking about?" replies the first.

"You've got to have *mud*," says the other. "See, first you spit into your hands, then you stoop down and get some dirt, and go to a pool and wash the mud from your. . . ."[1]

It is all too easy to argue about most of the aspects of the Person and work of the Holy Spirit and I am certain that Satan is delighted by all this controversy. The above story is humorous, but we must see that it describes an absolute tragedy.

For many years I have tried to reconcile the views of various people concerning the Holy Spirit. At times I have been happy over progress made; more often I have been discouraged. At one time I was the pastor of a very flexible church where we had wonderful times of open worship, and the charismatics were encouraged to hold home meetings and to exercise all the gifts. It was left to their discretion as to whom was invited. Despite this, the charismatics began to drop out of the church and to attend charismatic churches, even though no one could have been more sympathetic than the elders and myself. I know churches that have been able to integrate charismatic and non-charismatic Christians in their work and ministry. I have warm memories of visiting a Presbyterian church in Parksburg, Pa., where the Rev. James Brown has been the minister for many years. On Saturday nights they hold a charismatic meeting for praise and worship which is inspiring to attend. I have seen and heard nuns and priests sing and testify, as well as Mennonites with their distinctive dress. People of all ages attend and there are always many young people present. The meetings are lengthy but well under control. The services on Sunday morning could not be a greater contrast, being typically dignified and even staid "Presbyterian" services. Such churches are not uncommon, but to achieve harmony requires a great deal of love and flexibility on both sides.

One area where some of the greatest tensions have arisen

[1]Peter E. Gillquist, *Let's Quit Fighting About the Holy Spirit* (Grand Rapids: Zondervan, 1974), pp. 107-108.

has been on the mission field. Missionary leaders know that the most destructive force in their work is division; and some of the worst crises have occurred through missionaries who began to speak in tongues. The fault is by no means all one-sided. Some Christians that have received the gift of tongues not merely practiced it privately but aggressively propagated it. On the other hand, fellow missionaries sometimes lack the love and flexibility to adapt to it and can become bitter in their opposition.

Thought and prayer should be given to those who feel called to missionary work and who are charismatic. In most cases interdenominational missions are unwilling to accept them; and in many cases the would-be missionary does not feel at home in one of the Pentecostal denominations such as the Assemblies of God. In these circumstances the only alternative seems to be for the missionary to go out as an independent. This is indeed unsatisfactory for every missionary needs the training, language learning, fellowship, and supervision that can be provided only by an established mission.

Then there is the obvious fact that charismatic churches and non-charismatic churches need each other. As Paul points out, no Christian can say to another, "I have no need of you." The ordinary churches need the warmth and spontaneity of the charismatics; and they in turn need the teaching and guidance that should come from virile but noncharismatic churches. Often charismatics won't listen to a noncharismatic, and they become so cut off from all except charismatic speakers that they are virtually brainwashed.

When missionaries are sent overseas they usually are regarded as failures if they cannot adapt to bewildering changes of customs and procedures. What is needed today is that Christians at home would display some of that same flexibility.

The charismatic movement today presents the church of Christ with one of the greatest challenges it has known for many generations. It also offers an unparalleled opportunity for renewal. In such a situation Satan is bound to be working overtime. I am not one who has been given the gift of tongues, but I would insist that I have received the baptism of the Spirit and enjoy the fullness of the Spirit. I regard myself as a charismatic Christian in the sense that God in His love and grace has given me several gifts of the Spirit. I would ask my brothers in Christ to be careful lest we grieve the Holy Spirit by an attitude of divisiveness and criticism.

As I come to the close of this book my greatest concern is not that some should agree or disagree with what I have written, or even that some might have gained new insights into the work of the Holy Spirit. My prayer is that each reader will experience for himself the fullness of the Holy Spirit. The Lord is prepared to grant this to all who have been cleansed by sin after confession to the Lord, and have appropriated the gift of the fullness of the Holy Spirit. That is the heritage of each one of us who knows and loves the Lord Jesus Christ.

May this be the experience of many Christians so that we shall yet see a great and continuous revival in our time.

FOR DISCUSSION

1. Describe some difficulties in integrating charismatic Christians into a noncharismatic church.
2. Has the charismatic movement been a problem on the mission field?
3. Describe some difficulties of charismatic Christians who wish to become missionaries.
4. What is a definition of a charismatic Christian?
5. How can we become Spirit-filled Christians?

Bibliography

Basham, Don W. *Ministering the Baptism in the Holy Spirit* (Springdale: Whitaker Books, 1971).

Bennett, Dennis J. *Nine O'Clock in the Morning* (Plainfield, NJ: Logos International, 1970).

Bennett, Dennis and Rita. *The Holy Spirit and You* (Plainfield, NJ: Logos International, 1971).

Bitlinger, Arnold. *Gifts and Graces* (London: Hodder and Stoughton, 1973).

Bruner, Frederick Dale. *A Theology of the Holy Spirit* (Grand Rapids: Eerdmans, 1970).

Campbell, Thomas H. *Good News on the Frontier* (Memphis: Frontier Press, n.d.).

Christenson, Larry. *The Charismatic Renewal Among Lutherans* (Minneapolis: Bethany Fellowship, 1976).

_____. *A Charismatic Approach to Social Action* (Minneapolis: Bethany Fellowship, 1974).

_____. *Speaking in Tongues* (Minneapolis: Bethany Fellowship, 1968).

Cumming, J. Elder. *Through the Eternal Spirit* (London: Stirling Tract Enterprise, 1937).

Duncan, George B. *The Person and Work of the Holy Spirit in the Life of the Believer* (London: Lakeland, 1973).

Fife, Eric S. and Glasser, Arthur F. *Missions in Crisis* (Chicago: Inter-Varsity Press, 1961).

Flynn, Leslie B. *19 Gifts of the Spirit* (Wheaton: Victor Books, 1974).

Flynn, Thomas. *The Charismatic Renewal and Irish Experience* (London: Hodder and Stoughton, 1974).

Frost, Henry W. *Miraculous Healing* (London: Marshall, Morgan & Scott, 1951).

Gee, Donald. *Spiritual Gifts in the Work of the Ministry Today* (Springfield: Gospel Publishing House, 1963).

_____. *Now That You've Been Baptized in the Spirit* (Springfield: Gospel Publishing House, 1972).

_____. *The Fruit of the Spirit* (Springfield: Gospel Publishing House, 1975).

_____. *A New Discovery* (formerly printed as *Pentecost*: London, 1932).

Gelpi, Donald L. *Theology of Christian Conversion* (New York: Paulist Press, n.d.).

201

Gillquist, Peter E. *Let's Quit Fighting About the Holy Spirit* (Grand Rapids: Zondervan, 1974).

Green, Michael. *I Believe in the Holy Spirit* (Grand Rapids: Eerdmans, 1975).

Hammond, T. C. *In Understanding Be Men* (Leicester: InterVarsity Press, 1968).

Harper, Michael. *As at the Beginning* (London: Hodder & Stoughton, 1966).

Hathaway, W. G. *Spiritual Gifts in the Church* (London: Elim, 1933).

Horton, Harold. *The Gifts of the Spirit* (London: Assemblies of God Publishing House, 1962).

Howard, David M. *By the Power of the Holy Spirit* (Downers Grove: InterVarsity Press, 1973).

Hummel, Charles E. *Fire in the Fireplace* (Downers Grove: InterVarsity Press, 1977).

Kelsey, Morton T. *Speaking With Tongues* (London: Epworth Press, 1964).

Kendrick, Klaude. *The Promise Fulfilled* (Springfield, Mo.: Gospel Publishing House, 1961).

Kevan, Ernest F. *The Saving Work of the Holy Spirit* (London: Pickering & Inglis, 1953).

Law, William. *The Power of the Holy Spirit* (Fort Washington, Pa.: Christian Literature Crusade, 1971).

McDonnold, B. W. *History of the Cumberland Church,* 1888.

Morgan, G. Campbell. *The Spirit of God* (London: Westminster City Publishing, n.d.)

Morris, Leon. *Spirit of the Living God* (Chicago: InterVarsity Press, 1960).

Newbigin, L. *The Household of God* (Student Christian Movement, n.d.).

O'Connor, Edward D. *Pentecost in the Catholic Church* (Pecos, N.M.: Dove Publications, 1970).

Owen, John. *The Holy Spirit* (Grand Rapids: Sovereign Grace Publishers, n.d.).

Pache, René. *The Person and Work of the Holy Spirit* (Chicago: Moody Press, 1954).

Palmer, Edwin H. *The Person and Ministry of the Holy Spirit: The Traditional Calvinistic Perspective* (Grand Rapids: Baker Book House, 1974).

Phypers, Donald Bridge David. *Spiritual Gifts and the Church* (London: Inter-Varsity, 1973).

Ranaghan, Kevin and Dorothy. *Catholic Pentecostals* (New York: Paulist Press, 1969).

Salisbury, Roger. *The Holy Spirit Experience* (London: Lutterworth Press, 1973).

Sanders, J. Oswald. *The Holy Spirit and His Gifts* (Grand Rapids: Zondervan, 1940).

Scully, Jim. *The Catholic Pentecostal Movement* (Pecos, N.M.: Dove Publications, n.d.).

———. *Charismatic Renewal* (Pecos, N.M.: Dove Publications, n.d.).

Shakarian, Demos. *The Happiest People on Earth* (New York: Pillar Books, 1975).

Sherrill, John L. *They Speak With Other Tongues* (Lincoln, Va.: Chosen Books, 1964).

Smeaton, George. *The Holy Spirit* (London: Banner of Truth Trust, 1958).

Stott, John R. W. *Baptism and Fullness* (London: Inter-Varsity, 1964).

———. *The Baptism and Fullness of the Holy Spirit* (Downers Grove: InterVarsity, 1976).

Torrey, R. A. *The Person and Work of the Holy Spirit* (London: Nisbet, 1910).

Tozer, A. W. *The Knowledge of the Holy* (New York: Harper & Row, 1975).

Walvoord, John F. *The Holy Spirit at Work Today* (Chicago: Moody Press, 1973).

Webster, Douglas. *Pentecostalism and Speaking With Tongues* (London: Highway Press, 1964).

Wigglesworth, Smith. *Ever Increasing Faith* (Springfield, Mo.: Gospel Publishing House, 1971).

Wilkerson, David. *The Cross and the Switchblade* (Westwood, NJ: Spire, 1970).

Wogen, Norris L. *The Shadow of His Hand* (Minneapolis: Bethany Fellowship, 1975).

On Armenia

Arlen, Michael J. *Passage to Ararat* (New York: Ballantine, 1976).

Sarian, Nerses S. *I Shall Not Die* (London: Marshall, Morgan & Scott, 1967).

Shakarian, Demos. *The Happiest People on Earth* (Lincoln, Va.: Chosen Books, 1975).

Varjabedian, S. H. *The Armenians* (Chicago: Published privately, 1977).

SCRIPTURE INDEX

GENESIS
1:1, 2 25
1:2 .... 25, 26, 78
1:26 23
2:7 30
41:38 51

EXODUS
15:11 41
31:1-5 139
33:18-23 40
33:20 40
34:4-5 40
34:29-30 40

LEVITICUS
23:15-21 76

NUMBERS
11:25 52
27:18 51

DEUTERONOMY
16:16-17 160

JUDGES
13:2-5 52
13:25 52
14:5-6 52
14:19 52
15:14-15 52
16:17 53
16:20 53

1 SAMUEL
9:15-16 54
10:1 54
10:9-10 54
11:6 54
16:1 54
16:12 54
16:13-14 54
31:4 54

2 SAMUEL
12:1-18 128
12:13 55

1 KINGS
8:27 47

1 CHRONICLES
29:11-13 43

JOB
26:13 27
26:14 27
38:7 29
42:2 45

PSALMS
8:1 27
8:3, 9 28
8:5 31
8:5-8 30

33:6-7 27
51:10-11 55
62:11 44
104:1 28
104:2, 3 29
104:11 29
104:14 29
104:19 28
104:30 29
107:1, 8 46
139:6-12 47

PROVERBS
11:24-25 160

ISAIAH
6:1 41
6:1-5 41
11:2 37
40:7 30
40:13-14 38
48:16 39
59:20-21 57
61:1-2 70
63 19
63:10 19

EZEKIEL
2:2 56
11:5 56
11:19-20 56

JOEL
2:28-29 50
2:28-32 57

ZEPHANIAH
3:17 46

MATTHEW
1:18 66
1:20 66
3:11 96
3:16-17 .... 23, 68
4:1 69
6:3-4 160
7:28-29 129
11:2-6 64
11:11 64
12:28 71
12:31 20
12:31-32 20
12:32 71
17:1-2, 5 39
24:15-22 127
28:7, 10, 16 77
28:16-20 77
28:19 23
28:19-20 .... 81, 130

MARK
3:29 34
16:7 77

LUKE
1:26-35 67
2:40 68
2:46-47 68
3:16 145
4:1-2 69
4:14 70
4:14-21 69
4:18-19 70
4:20 70
4:21 70
10:17 78-79
16:16 65

JOHN
1:33-34 69
2:11 .... 26, 134
3:5-6 103
3:5-8 96
3:34-35 71
4:36-38 157
7:38-39 73
7:39 55
10:10 98
10:11 158
10:17-18 72
12:23-24 74
14:16-17 .... 18, 78
14:17 79
15:13 47
15:16 118
16:2-3 20
16:13-14 .... 18, 20,
 .... 37, 91
16:14 182
19:10 72
19:30 73
21:18-19 126

ACTS
1:8 .... 83, 91, 107
1:11 83
1:14 77
1:15 77
1:21-26 122
1:26 122
2:2 26
2:4 79
2:5 78
2:8-11 77
2:11 80
2:16-17 57
2:32 74
2:32-33 59
2:37-38 59
2:37-39 97
2:38-39 81
2:40 81
2:41 .... 58, 142
2:42 .... 81, 130

2:44-45   174
2:45   161
2:47   119
4:1-2   89
4:4   143
4:8   85
4:13   85
4:18   89
4:31   105
5:1-6   19
5:3-4   20
5:9   19, 20
5:13-14   91
5:16   91
6:3   85, 98, 120
6:7   91
6:10   85
7:24-25   44
7:51   20,62
8:1, 4-5   89
8:5   92
8:5-6   156
8:35   156
9:15   92
9:17-19   143
9:36-42   134
10:14-15   93
10:44-45   93
10:44-48   141
11:18   94, 142
11:19   92
11:20-21   92
11:27-28   126
12:6-11   134
13:1   124
13:2-3   169
13:22   56
15:36   169
16:6-10   168
16:33   143
17:34   143
19:1-6   142
19:10-20   143-144
21:4   127
21:8   156
24:21   90
27:34   86

ROMANS
1:16   44
1:20   26
1:20-21   33
5:12-14   51
7:18   103
8:8   103
8:9   96
8:11   75
8:26-27   39

8:28   45, 167
8:29   118
8:35-39   47
12:6-8   133
12:7   130
12:8   159

1 CORINTHIANS
1:21   36
1:25   44
2:9-11   37
2:10-11   20, 37
2:12-13   153
3:19, 20   36
4:2   159
6:9-10   167
6:19-20   60
12:4-13   111
12:7   109
12:8-9   152
12:9   154
12:10   154
12:13   96
12:28   124, 130, 134, 135, 138, 144, 148
12:28-30   113
12:28, 30   113
12:31   109, 110, 116, 148
13:1   150
13:1-14:1   117
13:5   157
13:8   124
13:10   124
14:1   109, 124, 131
14:2, 4   151
14:5   148
14:15   150, 151
14:18   148
14:26-33   113
14:27-28   150
14:29   128
14:32   113
14:39   109
14:39-40   148
15:5-8   121
15:14   74

2 CORINTHIANS
6:14   167
9:1-6   160
9:7   174
9:11, 12, 15   161
12:7-10   137

GALATIANS
1:19   122, 123
4:4   67

5:16   105
5:17   103
5:19-21   104, 120
5:22-23   118

EPHESIANS
3:17-19   45
4:11   124, 130, 155, 156, 157
4:11-15   158
4:17   36
4:30   20, 61
5:18   61, 80, 99
6:17   164

PHILIPPIANS
2:7   66
4:17   161

1 THESSALONIANS
1:5   86
5:19   20, 61, 105

2 THESSALONIANS
2:8   42
2:9   42

1 TIMOTHY
3:6   178
5:17-18   140

2 TIMOTHY
4:5   157
4:13   133
4:20   137

HEBREWS
1:3   73
3:1   123
9:9   72
9:14   72, 75
10:5   66
10:28-29   19, 20
13:20-21   158

JAMES
1:5   37
5:14-15   137

1 PETER
3:18   75
4:10-11   111

1 JOHN
4:1   155
4:8   20, 45
5:14   154

REVELATION
1:14, 15   40
1:16   40
1:17   35, 40
12:11   164
21:14   123

SUBJECT INDEX

Alexander, king 44
Ananias 19, 92, 98
Antichrist 62
Antiochus Epiphanes 127
Apostles: as gift of the Spirit 121-124
Apostolic church: Holy Spirit and 83-94; spread of 91-94
Apostles, message of 89-91
Armenian massacres 194
Armenian Pentecostals 194
Armenian story 192-194
As At the Beginning 185
Assemblies of God 108, 132, 133, 140, 187, 188, 195, 199
Attribute, definition of 35
Attributes of God: defaced by sin and disobedience 30; Puritans and, 34
Azusa Street, revival of 187-189

Baptism: of the Holy Spirit 95-97, 142; of Jesus Christ 68-71
Baptism and Fullness of the Holy Spirit, The 98, 112, 151
Baptism of the Holy Spirit: meaning of 95-97; not urged upon Christians 99; a once-for-all experience 102
Barclay, William 152
Baring-Gould, Sabine 45
Barnabas 122
Basham, Don W. 145-147
Bennett, Dennis J. 133-134, 177-178
Bennett, Rita 134
Bible: concern of 36; purpose of 33
Bible exposition, gift of 153
Binney, Thomas 41
Bonar, Horatius 89
Brown, James 198
Bull, Geofrey 60, 61
Bunyan, John 34

Calvin, John 183
Celestial bodies, movement of 28
Charismata 159; definition of 183
Charismatic movement: Armenian story and 192-194; Assemblies of God and 195; Lutheran church and 189-190; Roman Catholics and 191-192; sketch of 183-196; strengths of 170-175; weaknesses of 176-182
Charismatic Renewal Among Lutherans, The 189
Chinese Pentecostals 194

Christenson, Larry 189-190
Christian and Missionary Alliance 187
Christian Brethren 128, 170
Christian service, related to Holy Spirit 107-108
Christians: called to be soul winners 101; Spirit-oriented 17; witnessing of 101
Church, the; need in today, 86
Commentary on First Corinthians 139
Common grace: Holy Spirit and 60-63; meaning of 62
Cornelius 89, 93, 141
Cowper, William 34
Creation: of animals and vegetation 29-30; of the earth and ocean 25-27; of the heavens 27-29; Holy Spirit and 25-32; of man 30-31
Cumberland Presbyterian Church, the Charismatic movement and 185-187
Cumming, J. E. Elder 50

David 26-27, 28, 30-31, 44, 47, 53, 54, 55, 56, 128
Dearing, Trevor 165
Decline and Fall of the Roman Empire, The 45
Delilah 53
Discerning of spirits, as a gift to the church 154-155
Disciples, change in 84-89
Disobedience, separates from God 48
Divine healing, *see* Healing
Dorcas 134

Edwards, Jonathan 86-87, 185
Evangelicals: Christ's incarnation and, 67; knowledge of God and 33
Evangelism, as a gift of the Spirit 155-157
Exorcism, 163-166; dangers and errors of 164-166; diagnosis of 163-164; treatment of 164
Experience, in the Charismatic movement 177

Faith, as a gift of the Spirit 154
Faith healing, *see* Healing
Fall, the 30
Flesh, works of 104
Foursquare Church, beginning of 187
Francis, Samuel Trevor 46

Full Gospel Businessmen's Fellowship 139, 190, 193
Fullness of the Holy Spirit 98-102: charismatics and 100; urged for Christians 99
Gee, Donald 112, 119-120, 153, 167-168, 176, 180-181
Gelpi, Donald L. 153
Gibbon, Edward 45
Gillquist, Peter 197, 198
Glasser, Arthur 188, 194
God: as creator 25-32; attributes of 30; covenant-keeping 58; dealings with men 64; holiness of 39-43; limitless power of 43; nature of 18; philosophy and 36; separation from 48
God Holds the Key 61
God's Way of Holiness 89
Gospel the, spread of 94
Gospels, the: Holy Spirit in 64-75; period of 65; related to Old Testament 65
Grace Abounding 34
Graham Billy 107, 117, 118, 183
Great Awakening 185
Greek Orthodox Church 184
Green, Michael 128-129, 133, 150

Hammond, T. C. 74
Happiest People on Earth, The 193
Harper, Michael 185
Harris, Howell 87
Hathaway, W. G. 155
Healing, as gift of the Spirit 135-138
Helping, as gift of the Spirit 138-139
History of the Christian Church 184
History of the Cumberland Presbyterian Church 186
Hitler, Adolf 193; gas chambers of 44
Hodges, Melvin 132, 188, 195
Holiness: meaning of 40; spirit of 39-43; understanding of 40
Hollywood evangelism 117
Holy of Holies 73

Holy Spirit: apostolic church and 83-84; as Counselor 37; attributes of 33-49; baptism of 95-97; in Bible 62; blasphemy against 71; characteristics of 20-21; characteristics of work of 51; Christian service and 107-108; conflict between flesh and 104-105; creation and 25-32; divine guidance and 167-169; fruits of 116-120; fullness of 95, 98-102; gifts of 107-115, 116-120, 121-161; in the Gospels 64-75; honor due Him 34; knowledge of 38; likened to wind 26; in lives of believers 60, 104-106; love and 45-47; ministry concerning 50; need for authority of 88; need in church 61; neglect of what He does 17; no secrets from 37; Old Testament and 50-59; Pentecost and 76-82; person and work of 50; personality of 17-21; poured out 55; power of 71; prayer for 77; tenses of 50; the Trinity and 22-24, 35; unlimited presence of 47-48; work of 56, 58
Holy Spirit, The (Owen) 25
Holy Spirit, The (Smeaton) 50, 72
Holy Spirit and His Gifts, The 81
Holy Spirit and You, The 134
Holy Spirit at Word Today, The 110
Horoscopes, study of 28
Hound of Heaven, The 48
Human depravity, definition of 62
Hummel, Charles 188

I Believe in the Holy Spirit 129, 150
Immaculate Conception, doctrine of 67
In Understanding Be Men 74
Incarnation, the 65-68; as battleground 67; description of 66; mystery of 65
Isaiah 37, 38, 39, 41, 42

James (apostle) 37
James (the Lord's brother) 122-123
Jesus Christ: as divine instructor 37; baptism of 68-71; death of 72-74; deity of 67; humanity of 67; incarnation of 65-68; indwelt by Holy Spirit 71, 72; miracles of 26; public ministry of 71; resurrection of 74-75; in the synagogue 70; temptation of 69
Job 27, 45
Joel 50, 57, 81
John (apostle) 31, 35, 73, 85, 89
John the Baptist 64, 69, 96, 142
John XXIII, Pope 173, 191
Joseph 51, 52
Joseph (Jesus' father) 66
Joshua 51, 52
Jowett, Henry 130

Kelsy, Morton T. 15tn 184, 187
Kendrick, Klaude 187, 195
Klubniken, Efim Gerasemovitch 126

208

Knowledge: limitless 36-39; man and 36

Knowledge of the Holy, The 18, 42

Lasers, power of 44
Laying on of hands 137
Let's Quit Fighting About the Holy Spirit 198
Liberality, as a gift of the Holy Spirit 159
Love, of God 46
Luther, Martin 25, 183, 184
Lutheran Charismatic Renewal Services 189-190
Lutherans, and the Charismatic movement 189-190

McCheyne, Robert Murray 117
Man, creation of 30-31
Mary (Jesus' mother) 66-67
Matthias 122
Microwaves, power of 44
Miller, Perry 185
Ministering the Baptism in the Holy Spirit 147
Miracles, miracle workers and 133-135
Missions in Crisis 173, 188
Moody, Dwight L. 183
Morgan, G. Campbell 19, 77, 95-96
Morris, Leon 139, 152
Morris, Paul 188
Moses, 40, 42, 51, 52
Moss, Larry 186
Mueller, George 154
Muslims: Trinity and 22; work amongst 118

Narrative of Surprising Conversions in New England, A 87
Nathan 128
National Association of Evangelicals, founding of 188
Natural man, dead to things of God 62
Nazirite vow 53
New English Bible 26, 31, 42, 78, 104, 113, 134, 139, 140
New International Version of the Bible 159
Nicodemus 96
No Exit 48
Now That You've Been Baptized in the Spirit 119

Old Testament, Holy Spirit and 50
Omnipotence: of the Holy Spirit 43-45; sovereignty and 44

Omniscience: meaning of 36; quality of knowledge and 38
Operation Mobilization 154
Orthodox Armenian Church 193
Owen, John 25, 65, 72

Pache, Rene 55
Packer, James 62
Palmer, Edwin 62
Passover: feast of 76; linked to Pentecost 76; week 76
Pastoring, as a gift of the Spirit 157-159
Paul 33, 34, 37, 42, 44, 45, 47, 86, 90, 92, 96, 103-104, 111, 113, 116, 118-119, 121-124, 129, 132, 135, 137, 139, 142-144, 150-152, 165, 168-169, 177, 178, 199
Pentecost: as birth of the church 79; changes in Peter and 84; description of 76; as division between Old Testament and New Testament 64; events of 83; Holy Spirit and 76-82; speaking in tongues and 141, 142
Pentecostal movement 119, 148; writings of 133-134
Person and Ministry of the Holy Spirit, The 62
Person and Work of the Holy Spirit, The 55
Peter 57, 58, 59, 75, 81, 84-85, 89, 93, 97, 98, 112, 122-124, 126, 134, 135, 141
Pharaoh 51
Philip 89, 92, 156
Phillips, J. B. 66, 81, 118, 134, 157, 160, 174
Philosophy: concern of 36; God and 36
Pilgrim's Progress 34
Pilate, Pontius 72
Praying, for healing 136
Prince, Derek 145
Promise Fulfilled, The 187, 195
Prophecies: fulfillment of 70; inspired by the Holy Spirit 56; need for 124; will pass away 124
Prophets: as forecaster 125-127; as forthteller 127-129; gift of Spirit 121-129; work of 56
Pseudo-psychology 177
Puritans: Holy Spirit and 35; preaching of 34

Repentance, of David 55
Revised Standard Version of the Bible 26, 134, 139, 140, 153

Revival: in history 86-87; in Massachusetts 86-87; in our day, 42; Welsh 87
Richard, Clif 178
Roman Catholics, the Charismatic movement and 191-192
Ruling elders 140
Russian Pentecostals 194

Samsom 52, 53, 54, 55, 56
Samuel 54, 55
Sanders, J. Oswald 80-81
Sapphira 19, 98
Sartre, Jean-Paul 48
Satan, purpose of 33
Saul 53, 54
Second Awakening 186
Shadow of His Hand, The 190
Shakarian, Demos 139, 192-194
Sherrill, John L. 149
Simpson, A. B. 187
Sin: repentance of 55-56; sensitivity to 56
Smeaton, George 50, 72
Smith, Walter Chambers 23
Solomon 47
Speaking With Tongues 184
Spirit of God, The 19, 96
Spiritual gifts: administration 139-140; apostles 121-124; different views of 109; discerning of spirits 154-155; evangelism 155-157; faith 154; for today 108-112; healing 135-138; helping 138-139; human personalities and 113-114; liberality 159-161; lists of 111; natural talents and 112-113; origin of 114; pastoring and teaching 157-159, 176; prophets 124-129; teachers 129-133; tongues 140-152; utterance 152-153; working of miracles 133-135
Spiritual Gifts in the Church 155
Spiritual Gifts in the Life of the Ministry Today 112, 168, 176, 181
Spiritual warfare 103-106
Spurgeon, C. H. 18, 108, 183
Stephen 19-20, 62, 85, 89, 92
Stott, John R. W. 98, 109, 112, 151
Suenes, Cardinal 191
Sung, John 119

Taylor, Hudson 154

Teaching, gift of 110, 129-133, 157-159, 176
Teaching elders 140
Tertullian 184
They Speak With Other Tongues 149
Thompson, Francis 48
Through the Eternal Spirit 50
Timothy 178
Titus, Emperor 127
Tongues: as evidence of Spirit baptism 141-148; definition of 113; for today? 148-149; gift of 71, 80-81, 100, 110, 112, 140-154; help from 149-152; Pentecost and 79; in private devotions 150; in public meetings 150; purpose of 80; types of 150
Touryan, Kenell 192-194
Touryan, Vahram 192-194
Tozer, A. W. 17, 18, 38, 42, 48
Trinity, the: at Christ's baptism 68; holiness as attribute of 42; Holy Spirit and 22-24; 33; Persons of 23; unity of 35
Troutman, Charles 188
Twelve, the 122-123

Unforgivable sin, 34
Union Theological Seminary 188
Unitarians, The Trinity and 22
U.S. News and World Report 195
Unlimited power, concept of 44
Utterance, as gift of the Holy Spirit 152-153

Van Dusen, Henry 188
Vatican II 191
Verwer, George 154
"Victorious life," meaning of 101

Walsh, Thomas 184
Walvoord, John 109-110
Welsh Revival 184
Wesley, Charles 90, 173
Wesley, John 90, 183, 184, 185
Whitefield, George 86-87, 183
Whittier, John Greenleaf 46
Witnessing: evangelism and, 101; soul-winning and 101
Wogen, Norris L. 190
Wycliffe Bible translators 149
Wycliffe, John 183

Yale Divinity School 188

Zephaniah 46